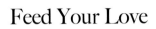

Feed Your Love

Divine Nectar of Papaya *(recipe on p. 127)*

Feed Your Love

122 Recipes from Around the World to Spice Up Your Love Life

GUILLERMO FERRARA

TRANSLATED BY: TIMOTHY BARALIS

Skyhorse Publishing

Contents

Introduction.. 11
Foods That Improve Your Sexual Vitality..................................... 15

THE ART OF COOKING WITH LOVE

Feelings and Food.. 34
A Matter of Health... 34
Food and Sexual Desire.. 35
Yin Foods, Yang Foods... 36
Balanced Eating... 37
Food and Repression... 38
Destruction, Creation, and Preservation.................................... 39
Processing Your Food as Well as Your Relationships......................... 39
Are We What We Eat, or What We Digest?.................................... 40
Foods That Awaken Sexuality... 42
Rituals for The Beloved... 43
Cooking Up Love in the Kitchen.. 48
Cooking and the Chakras... 49
Cooking for People on the Go.. 49

GREEK RECIPES

Light Aphrodisiac Suppers...... 52
Luminous Greek Lunches,
    Snacks, and Hors d'oeuvres.... 57
Savory, Spicy Dishes........... 63
Recipes for Ardent Lovers....... 71
Flirty Fish Recipes 79
Mediterranean Delights 85

HINDU RECIPES

Power Breakfasts and Light
    Meals....................... 95
Recipes That Arouse Passion... 106
Salads, Chicken, and Casseroles ..117
Desserts and Sweets 125

MAYAN AND AZTEC RECIPES

Chocolate Temptations....... 133
Spicy Mexican Recipes........ 139

MISCELLANEOUS RECIPES

Bread, Fish, and Lamb......... 145

Dedication

To the spirit of the primal goddess.

And to those gods that are always before the face of those who are awake.

Above all, to Dionysus, Apollo, and Shiva. And especially to the goddess Kali,
Who protects me and grants my desires.

To those women who radiate divinity with their simple presence.

To those who are not bound by limiting beliefs and mechanical traditions,
But are guided by the connection of the human heart with the divine
Through direct knowing.

To those who know there is but one, nameless God/Goddess
Of myriad forms, as a tree has but one trunk
But gives forth many branches and many fruits.

From my Buddha Nature.

My Thanks

To those who taught me to cook with love and finesse: my mother Carmen,
Mariela, Eliana, and Heidie. Goddesses of the arts of love and the kitchen.

Introduction

With life's first breath a human being draws in vitalizing energy. This air is our first food and mother's milk is our second. Later on come the foods lovingly prepared by mother. In my country, Argentina, family meals are very important, a daily celebration based on dishes made with great care and devotion, dishes which offer a delight of different tastes and textures.

The pace of life today, however, has dealt us a bad hand. We always eat away from home, a bad habit and serious emotional deprivation which turns the magic of dining into an act of mere survival.

In ancient times, dining was synonymous with festal thanksgiving to Earth/ Gaia for giving us nurture. Nowadays, we eat thinking about business, our job, sports, etc. We no longer *savor* our food, we just go through the process of eating, ever distracted by thousands of things. Very old and wise Eastern cultural traditions, such as yoga, advise us to chew thoroughly so that the digestive enzymes can properly initiate digestion. But today the majority of us end up gulping down our food, almost without chewing, simply to satisfy the primal animal instinct of survival.

Disappearing, too, is the custom of inviting friends and family over to dine in our homes. Instead, we make reservations at a restaurant. Sure, you don't have to wash the dishes or be bothered with cooking or worry about how your house looks, but you are thus deprived of the joy of cooking for your loved ones and thereby experiencing a ritual of celebration which allows you to offer your love and mirth via your personal preparation of the meal.

With this book I invite all of you to enjoy celebratory cooking and regain the pleasures of dining and the inner art of expressing your soul through cuisine.

The act of cooking is a form of play, something enjoyable, and a celebration. I, myself, begin with a cup of wine in hand, listening to Greek music—dynamic sirtaki dancing—or the Three Tenors or Demis Roussor. And believe me, it makes my spirit soar. It is a divine gift. To experience the culinary event unfolding joyfully is priceless. You awaken your senses. It is a canvas painted in colors and flavors and smells that intoxicate and carry you aloft to the inspired realization that life is something to celebrate and not mere drudgery.

Life's focus changes when you cook. You are arousing your senses with music, drinking, tastes, textures, aromas, colors, combinations, all beckoning you to a world of delight. I've always held that cooking is one of the most surefire ways of showing one's love. It is a life-giving act.

A scientist friend of mine once said that love is gestated in the kitchen. A kitchen has its own special atmosphere that radiates intimacy, as if it were a kind of womb where a lovingly prepared meal comes to full term. I have another friend who never has anything in his refrigerator. You can tell a lot about a person in numerous ways: body language (it never lies), with diagnostic tests, by their thinking, facial expressions, etc., but also by what they have in their icebox and how they feed themselves.

As I said earlier, in this book I invite you to engage in the spiritual aspect of cooking in a fun, healthy, and invigorating way. Even just cooking up a romantic supper with the object of seducing your partner, prepared in a sublime ambience of candles, music, and aromas that open the heart, will provide a beautiful pretext for showing your love, without having to say a word, but simply with dishes that can remove any emotional barriers between you and your companion. All of the recipes presented here originate from my mother, intimate companions, travels through Greece, Mexico, and India, as well as the expert help of my editor.

To cook is to celebrate, to delight, and to enjoy. It is a matter of sharing our joy, our caring, and our affection in the guise of a good meal. It is exactly in this way that our grandmothers and mothers would add that extra dose of love that so well nourished not only our bodies, but our hearts as well.

Let's get away from fast foods, pizza, and "ready-to-eat" meals. Wise sustenance promotes balance and harmony.

Let us allow food to be a way of thanksgiving and a tribute to those greater forces that enliven us, those forces that we don't always recognize due to the blindness of our fossilized beliefs. If you let them, these forces will totally open to you, day by day. They represent the fragrance of your experience and the savoring of the most important dish you could ever cook: your own life.

Guillermo Ferrara
Barcelona

Foods That Improve Your Sexual Vitality

Our sexual vitality depends on many factors, from the balance of our sexual hormones to our emotional state, or possible health problems, just to mention three of the most important.

Food is another of those aspects that stand out regarding sexual health; not just those foods that we consume, but also the nutritional standard we maintain. These will have a major effect on our enjoyment and betterment of sex. It is not advisable, for example, to overeat or skip any food: this will only result in feeling more fatigued or less *motivated* sexually.

Throughout this book we have presented numerous aphrodisiac recipes that will help you enjoy sex to the maximum. In this chapter we will discuss the foods—some well-known, others not so much—that contain nutrients, minerals, and vitamins that are our best allies for a healthy and satisfactory sex life.

Shrimp and Prawns
Calcium, iodine, magnesium, selenium, zinc.

As with all seafood, shrimp and prawns contain an abundance of zinc, magnesium, calcium, iodine, and selenium. They are also rich in the amino acid *phenylalanine*, commonly found in proteins, and vital for production of cerebral neurotransmitters that regulate our emotional stability and sexual appetite.

Tuna
Essential omega-3 fatty acids, selenium, zinc, vitamin B.

Tuna is one of the foods most beneficial to our sexual vitality. It is rich in zinc, selenium, vitamins B12 and B3, as well as omega-3 fatty acids. Frequent consumption of tuna elevates the sperm count, increases libido, and heightens sexual stamina.

Most Common Sexual Complaints of Men

The loss of sexual desire in a man can be the result of many things: stress, cardiovascular problems, or emotional issues, all of which negatively affect the production of testosterone. This is the hormone that is decisive in maintaining adequate libido and is present in both men and women.

Testosterone is vital to the production of sperm, fertility, and erectile function. A healthy man produces approximately 7 mg of testosterone daily. In cases where production of testosterone is below this, a man is liable to feel easily fatigued and suffer from loss of sexual desire. To compensate for lack of testosterone it is recommended to consume foods rich in zinc and vitamin B6.

More recently, it has been verified that inflammation of the prostate may affect erectile function. From a nutritional standpoint, it is a good idea to not over-consume foods rich in saturated fats (red meats, dairy products) and foods that result in increased blood glucose levels.

The body needs fats, but it is better to choose foods rich in essential fatty acids such as bluefish, dried fruits and oils, flax seed, and olive oil. In addition, zinc is a mineral that furthers prostate health.

Similarly, drugs such as *Viagra* increase blood flow to the penis and, as a result, facilitate erectile activity. It is no wonder this has become a very popular drug for millions of men throughout the world. However, it is not without its side effects and is not recommended for those who suffer from hypertension.

There are alternatives to *Viagra,* such as Siberian ginseng, yerba mate, yohimbine, sarsaparilla, and saw palmetto, the latter also being used for prostate difficulties. The natural product most equivalent to Viagra is *arginine,* an amino acid found in most animal products, and in popcorn!

Caviar

Iron, magnesium, and vitamin B (choline).

Caviar, fresh sturgeon eggs seasoned with salt, has been considered a delicacy since remote times (due in part to its rarity). It contains magnesium, iron, and *choline*, a type of vitamin B.

Sea Bass

Magnesium, essential omega-3 acids, selenium, and zinc.

Whitefish is very rich in omega-3, zinc, magnesium and selenium, all of which support sperm production and sexual drive.

Tofu

Calcium, iron, magnesium, phytoestrogens, vitamin A.

This food, whose beneficial properties have been known in the Orient for hundreds of years, contains phytoestrogens, substances that imitate the effects of natural estrogen. In this way, they help regulate the feminine hormonal balance.

In many Asian countries, women have fewer hormonal difficulties than occur with women in the West, due to the fact that they eat a lot of tofu. In addition, tofu is rich in iron, calcium, magnesium, and vitamin A.

Most Common Sexual Complaints of Women

In women, loss of desire is usually a hormonal problem. Both males and females produce testosterone and when there is a deficit of this hormone, it can result in loss of libido. This can be compensated for by consuming foods rich in zinc and vitamin B6. Another common problem involves an imbalance between estrogen and progesterone, causing a disruption of the menstrual cycle. Nowadays, it is more likely that a woman has excess estrogen due to environmental and dietary factors. Other factors, such as tobacco, stress, and antidepressants, can also negatively affect sexual function. Menopause and birth also cause imbalances in the female hormones, and this can result in loss of libido as well.

There are natural substances that amply compensate for declining desire. Some of them are vitamin A, vitamin B, vitamin C, E, chrome, and boron.

Sesame Seeds

Calcium, iron, magnesium omega-3, -6 acids, selenium, zinc, vitamin E.

These seeds are an indispensable part of a diet designed to maintain and improve our sexual vigor. They contain selenium, zinc (which combats  infertility), calcium, iron, magnesium, vitamin E, omega-3 and omega-6 essential fatty acids.

One can use sesame oil as a dressing, but should never heat it lest it lose its properties. Remember to chew the seeds slowly so that you can obtain the greatest benefit from the essential minerals they contain.

Brown Rice

Calcium, iron, magnesium, zinc, vitamin B.

Brown rice contains many ingredients related to sexual enhancement such as zinc, iron, magnesium, chrome, manganese, and calcium. There are many ways to prepare brown rice. It is excellent in a risotto, or as an accompaniment to meat or fish.

Rye

Calcium, iron, magnesium, zinc, vitamins B and E.

Rye contains many minerals directly implicated in healthy sexual function such as iron, magnesium, zinc, vitamins B5 and B6 (mood regulators), calcium, and vitamin E. In addition, its levels of phosphorus, magnesium, and silicon support higher levels of cerebral energy.

Popcorn

Arginine.

Popcorn is a source of arginine, an amino acid that is found mostly in meats. It is most important in the development, quantity, and quality of sperm. It is essential that vegan men add this food to their diet to maintain their fertility.

Pine Nuts

Calcium, magnesium, zinc, vitamin B.

Dried fruit and seeds are an indispensable source of protein in the vegetarian diet. These provide the essential building blocks for healthy sexual function. Specifically, pine nuts contain many minerals, especially zinc and magnesium as well as vitamin B and calcium. All of these vitamins help to maintain high levels of energy and sexual vigor.

Mango
Beta-carotene, vitamin C.

This delicious tropical fruit is very rich in beta-carotene, essential for production of both testosterone and estrogen. Mangoes also contain great quantities of vitamin C, which helps prevent sperm from becoming entangled.

Cheese
Arginine, calcium, magnesium, zinc.

Cheese contains vital nutrients for sexual health, such as arginine, calcium magnesium, and zinc (only seafood contains more zinc than cheese).

Almonds
Calcium, magnesium, omega-3, -6, zinc, vitamins B and E.

This delicious nut is rich in magnesium and one of the essential fatty acids that regulates prostaglandins (physiologically active substances present in many tissues, genital fluids, and ductile glands), vital for production of sex hormones. It also contains calcium, zinc, folic acid, and vitamins B2, B3, and E. Almonds are a wonderful ally for combating infertility and greatly help to increase libido.

Eggs
Calcium, iron, zinc, vitamin B.

All varieties of eggs (chicken, duck, quail, etc.) contain iron, zinc, calcium, vitamin B, and large amounts of protein. Organic eggs are always preferable. The yolks, above all, contain most of an egg's nutrients.

Papaya
Beta-carotene, calcium, magnesium, vitamin C.

Papaya contains large quantities of beta-carotene and vitamin C, as does mango. The seeds, also very nutritious, provide supplementary essential fatty acids that stimulate the production of sexual hormones. Papaya is also rich in calcium and magnesium. Its pulp is delicious with lime juice; you can leave in the seeds when you blend it.

Blackberries and Raspberries
Beta-carotene, calcium, magnesium, vitamins C and E.

These delicious, small fruits are an important source of vitamin C and vitamin E, fundamental in increasing libido and, also, helping to maintain smooth skin.

Both blackberries and raspberries are rich in calcium, magnesium, and beta-carotene.

Plums
Calcium, iron.

Plums are very rich in iron and calcium and provide phytoestrogens, which support hormonal balance in women. Plums also aid in digestion.

Strawberries
Beta-carotene, calcium, iron, magnesium, vitamins C and E.

This versatile fruit, that we can enjoy as a dessert, in a salad, or smoothie, possesses nutrients that help invigorate our sex life. Strawberries are an excellent source of vitamin C, iron (easily absorbed thanks to vitamin C!), beta-carotene, folic acid, vitamin E, calcium, and magnesium.

Bananas
Beta-carotene, magnesium, tryptophan, vitamin C.

Many times, decrease in libido is the result of emotional issues, such as mood swings or depression. The flesh of the banana closest to its peel contains an alkaloid named bufotenine that plays a role in maintaining the equilibrium of cerebral neurotransmitters; fostering emotional stability, self-esteem, and self-confidence. This certainly furthers healthier sexual vitality. In addition, bananas are rich in beta-carotene and vitamin C.

Figs
Beta-carotene, calcium, vitamin C.

Figs are the fruit most known for their aphrodisiac qualities. Their high content of beta-carotene insures regular production of sex hormones in the human body.

They are also a magnificent source of vitamin C, which increases libido and reduces stress. Figs are also an excellent source of calcium.

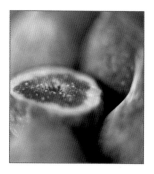

Avocado

Beta-carotene, essential fatty acids, iron, vitamins B and E.

Avocados contain vitamins B6 and E, essential for sexual vitality. When there is a deficit of these, the result is often sexual listlessness and lower fertility. Avocados also furnish iron, beta-carotene, folic acid, and vitamin B3.

Asparagus

Beta-carotene, vitamins B and C.

Asparagus contain numerous nutrients of benefit to our health, such as folic acid, beta-carotene, and vitamin C. They are also very helpful regarding liver health and, as a result, support hormonal balance if there is any imbalance of testosterone or estrogen production. Asparagus are a natural tonic and stimulate the sex drive.

Celery

Beta-carotene, selenium, group B vitamins.

In the Orient, celery root is valued for its aphrodisiac qualities; a result of folic acid, beta-carotene, and vitamin B6 being in combination. Celery is also rich in selenium. Selenium stimulates the pituitary gland, the "master gland" that regulates the endocrine system and production of sexual hormones.

Remember, too, that celery aids digestion, and helps prevent lowering of sexual desire due to have a bit too much to eat!

Tomatoes

Beta-carotene, calcium, magnesium, vitamins A, B, and C.

Vitamin A is indispensable for production of male and female sex hormones and promotes fertility. Tomatoes are rich in beta-carotene, the precursor of vitamin A, converted into same in the lining of the intestine. They are also an excellent anti-oxidant, supporting a healthy heart, something that obviously affects one's sexual stamina.

Onions and Leeks

Beta-carotene, calcium, chrome, and magnesium.

Onions and leeks are highly beneficial to the liver, an organ of great importance regarding feminine sexual health due to the fact that estrogens (the female sexual hormones) are synthesized there. Onions and leeks are rich in calcium and folic acid and are an excellent source of magnesium and beta-carotene, helping to maintain feminine hormonal balance and, above all, aid those women who suffer from severe premenstrual cramping or are going through menopause. It has also been confirmed that onions and leeks support male sexual function.

Lentils

Calcium, manganese, magnesium, zinc, vitamin B.

Lentils are a great help in supporting a healthy libido since they provide group B vitamins, zinc, manganese, calcium, and magnesium. One way to take advantage of lentils' libido-stimulating properties is to combine them in a *dahl*, a typical Indian dish that is a purée made of lentils, garlic, and onions.

Mushrooms and Truffles

Calcium, iron, magnesium, zinc, vitamin B.

Mushrooms are an excellent source of B vitamins and rich in calcium, iron, magnesium, and zinc.
You can prepare them many ways, using them raw in salads or cooked. For many years, truffles have been considered to be excellent aphrodisiacs, due to their distinctive odor and rarity. They are very expensive and, if this is an issue, can be substituted for by truffle oil, a much cheaper alternative.

Spinach

Beta-carotene, calcium, co-enzyme Q-10, iron, magnesium, vitamins B and C.

Raw spinach is one of the few greens that has co-enzyme Q10. It is also one of the most important sources of iron and provides folic acid, beta-carotene, vitamins B3 and B6, vitamin C, calcium, and magnesium.

Garlic

Calcium, vitamin C.

Since the Middle Ages, it has been known that garlic supports blood circulation and keeps the arteries clean. Hardening of the arteries is one of the principal causes of male impotence. Garlic helps support erectile function. It also contains calcium and vitamin C.

Beets

Beta-carotene, calcium, iron, potassium, vitamin C.

Beets improve function of the liver, where sexual hormones are balanced. They contain large amounts of beta-carotene and vitamin C, and are an excellent source of iron, calcium, and potassium, necessary for maintaining adequate blood circulation.

Pumpkin

Calcium, iron, magnesium, essential fatty acids omega-3 and omega-6, vitamin B.

Pumpkin seeds contain calcium, iron, magnesium zinc, vitamin B, and essential fatty acids omega-3 and omega-6 that are essential for the production of sex hormones (testosterone in the case of males). Omega-3 and omega-6 also have anti-inflammatory properties that help prevent prostate enlargement. Pumpkin is delicious raw, or lightly grilled with olive oil and soy sauce, in salads, or in soups.

Watercress

Beta-carotene, calcium, iron, magnesium, vitamin C.

This slightly bitter herb, delicious as a salad ingredient, is a rich source of iron and potassium (both indispensable for heart and circulatory health), calcium, beta-carotene, magnesium, and vitamin C. Watercress is a tonic and helps purify the blood, which is recommended for men who suffer from erectile dysfunction due to cardiac issues.

Broccoli

Iron, vitamins B and C.

Broccoli is considered to be the one vegetable never to be missed in our diets due to the fact that it is a cancer preventative, among its other benefits. It is also a strong source of iron, vitamin B, vitamin A and C (the last two principally and primarily anti-oxidants), giving it an important role to play in sexual health.

Cream

Arginine, calcium, vitamin B.

Cream is an excellent source of calcium and one of the favorite accompaniments for desserts and sweets; especially delicious with chocolate. It provides great amounts of vitamin B and arginine.

Dark Chocolate

Magnesium, phenylalanine, potassium.

Chocolate, due to its magnesium content, is a food that helps to prevent muscular cramps and premenstrual pain. It helps to improve the sexual vitality of many women.

Phenylalanine is a mood enhancer and helps to prevent emotional swings, which certainly helps one enjoy sex more!

Herbs and Spices: Boosters of Your Sexual Vigor

Raw or cooked, there are many aromatic herbs and spices that are beneficial for our health and sexual vigor. For example, **saffron** (the most expensive spice in the world) is famous for its aphrodisiac qualities. Keep in mind, however, that the only variety of saffron that helps boost male libido is *Crocus sativus,* which is grown only in Asia at specific times of the year.

Tarragon, for its part, is a heart and liver tonic (and so supports synthesis of estrogen and testosterone, the sex hormones) and is also a great blood purifier. **Nutmeg** is an important sexual stimulant, though it is necessary to remember that it can be highly toxic to our bodies if overused. In the seventeenth century this commodity was so prized that the English and Dutch fought over control of its trade. **Basil** is another sexual enhancer that has relaxing, anti-stressful properties. **Pesto** is a wonderful sauce that combines the stimulating properties of basil, pine nuts, and garlic; a great complement for many pasta dishes. You can prepare a dressing, delicious as it is healthy for your sex life, by tincturing olive oil with tarragon and basil leaves.

Lastly, **ginger** helps prevent blood thickening, and so supports erectile function. It contains beta-carotene, vitamin C, iron, zinc, and magnesium. It is also an aphrodisiac known from ancient times. It can be consumed alone, as a delicious tea, or can be added to a great variety of dishes.

Nutrients and Vitamins That Support Sexual Health

Zinc

Zinc is the most important mineral for our sexual health and fertility. Zinc helps provide sperm with their peculiar capacity for mobility. Zinc influences the health and production of sperm; about 5 mg of zinc are contained in a man's ejaculation.

For proper development of the sexual organs during puberty, it is necessary that adequate levels of zinc are available to our bodies. Zinc also is a necessary mineral that supports proper functioning of our senses of taste and smell, obviously important for sexual enjoyment.

Rich Sources: Seafood, in general (oysters and sardines in particular), eggs, cheese, lamb, chicken, turkey, liver, beef, brown rice, lentils, pumpkin, sesame seeds, spirulina, and whole grains.

Magnesium

Magnesium is another mineral indispensable for balancing sexual hormones and regulating the heartbeat. It plays an important role in energy production and, therefore, sexual vigor. It is vital for sexual sensitivity, sexual awakening, and supports ejaculation and orgasm.

Rich Sources: Green leafy vegetables, dried fruit, cheese, bananas, whole grains, caviar, and seafood.

Iron

Hemoglobin transports oxygen to all the cells of our bodies, thus producing energy.

Iron is fundamental to the production of hemoglobin. Energy is necessary for us to be able to function in any capacity, including sex. In addition, we need iron to absorb vitamin C, since our bodies are not capable of storing it and must consume what we need on a daily basis.

Rich Sources: Liver, red meat, chicken, caviar, grapes, plums, apricots, egg yolks, whole grains, watercress, spinach, broccoli, beets, and legumes. Remember that our bodies assimilate iron from animal sources better than that from plant sources.

Calcium

Calcium is fundamental for normal functioning of neural transmitters and the sense of touch, so important in sexual contact. In addition, many muscular movements associated with sexual function, such as erection of the penis, or contraction of the vaginal labia and other areas during female orgasm, require adequate levels of calcium.

Rich Sources: Dairy products, green leafy vegetables, beans, beets, watercress, plums, dried fruit, seafood, small fish (such as sardines and smelts).

Iodine

The thyroid gland is in charge of metabolic regulation, production of energy and hormones. If the thyroid malfunctions, there will be an inevitable loss of libido. Iodine is required for our bodies to produce thyroxin for proper thyroid function.

Rich Sources: Seafood, algae, kelp, and others (especially those of green-blue color), spirulina, watercress, beets, turnips (greens included), fruit juices, watermelon, cucumbers, spinach, and okra.

Boron

Boron is a trace element fundamental in the production of the sex hormones. When ingested in minute quantities, it increases the available levels of estrogen and testosterone.

Rich Sources: All greens, fruits, and vegetables.

Selenium

Selenium is essential for production of sperm and supports fertility. People who live in areas where there is a deficit of selenium in the soil should take selenium supplements to support their sexual health.

Rich Sources: Seafood, sesame and pumpkin seeds, Brazil nuts, butter, liver, and kidneys.

Chrome

Chrome is important in the production of insulin, which regulates blood sugar levels. Insulin also plays an important role in energy production. Lack of chrome can affect our energy level and libido.

Rich Sources: Soy products, brewer's yeast, cucumbers, onions, and garlic.

Arginine

Arginine is an amino acid found in protein. It plays an important part in sexual development and, specifically, supports sperm vitality.

Rich Sources: All animal products, including dairy products; popcorn (contains the highest levels of arginine in vegetable protein).

Co-enzyme Q10

Co-enzyme Q10 is an indispensable nutrient supporting energy production on the cellular level of our bodies. It is necessary to maintain adequate levels of co-enzyme Q10 and to keep in mind that as we age our body produces less of it.

Rich Sources: All animal foods, blue-green algae, chlorella (contained in all green-leaf vegetables), spinach, sardines, and peanuts.

Essential Fatty Acids

The essential fatty acids are not produced by our bodies and must be obtained through the diet. There are two types: omega-3 and omega-6. They play an important role in maintaining hormonal equilibrium, neuronal function, and healthy skin.

Rich Sources of Omega-3: Fish and seafood, sesame, pumpkin, and sunflower seeds and their oils.

Rich Sources of Omega-6: Avocadoes, pumpkin, sunflower, sesame, flax, hemp seeds and their oils.

Vitamin A

Vitamin A is a fundamental anti-oxidant that supports heart and cardio-vascular health. Vitamin A is vital to sexual health and can be found in beta-carotene or retinol. Vitamin A is essential for eye health (specifically vision) and supports strong bones and teeth. It is important for joint function and cartilage.

Rich Sources of Beta-Carotene: Green-leaf vegetables (dark green are best), including curly kale, Swiss chard, spinach, watercress, broccoli, parsley, as well as orange-yellow vegetables and fruits, such as cantaloupe melon, peaches, and tomatoes.

Rich Sources of Retinol: Pork and calf liver, dairy products, eggs, and oily fish.

Group B Vitamins (B1, B2, B3, B5, B6, B12, and Choline)

The B vitamins are vital for our body's energy production and digestion of carbohydrates. For example, vitamin B3 helps improve blood circulation (which helps erectile function) and stimulates production of histamine, a hormone that furthers orgasm.

Vitamin B6 is involved in production and release of the sexual hormones and reducing levels of prolactin (a hormone that causes milk secretion in women). It also is involved in regulating testosterone levels in men. Deficiencies in testosterone are

found in men going through andropause, the male equivalent of menopause.

Although choline is not strictly a vitamin, it is included in this group. It is the precursor of acetylcholine, a neuro-transmitter important in maintaining energy levels and healthy libido.

<u>Rich Sources:</u> Blackberries, blueberries, cherries, citrus fruits, kiwi, mangoes, papaya, figs, potatoes, green peppers, broccoli, beets, and sprouts (such as bean, lentil, soy, and alfalfa sprouts).

Vitamin E

Vitamin E is a powerful anti-oxidant that works in conjunction with vitamin C. It provides many beneficial properties and, regarding sexual health, protects the internal tissues associated with sexual vitality.

<u>Rich Sources:</u> All green-leaf vegetables, including broccoli, watercress, spinach, parsley, curly kale, avocado (contains one of the highest levels of vitamin E among plant foods), brown rice, dried fruits and their oils, oats, and wheat germ.

The Art of Cooking with Love

The human body requires nutrients: proteins, amino acids, fats, and carbohydrates. Vital energy is provided by food, water, and sunlight. By proper combining of various foods, we ensure a proper balance of vitalizing fuels.

It is our intention that the dishes and recipes we offer here be aphrodisiac and supporting of the life energy, which is none other than the *sexual energy*.

It is quite possible a couple is unaware of the fact that the woman needs to eat certain "Yin" foods so she continues to "vibrate" in a way that attracts her man. And the man, for his part, must eat certain "Yang" foods to magnetize his energy body so that he attracts his woman. Later on we will share a list of "Yin" and "Yang" foods to guide you in this.

Whatever feelings move you, whatever feelings you wish to express in the food you are preparing will provide the motivation for cooking. To cook out of obligation becomes a colorless affair, a matter of mere discipline, whereas a certain kind of "letting go" brings color and life to your cuisine, transforming it into a joyous activity and allowing the possibility of love to grace its preparation.

This is a form of alchemy wherein one's deep feelings *transform* the food and an atmosphere of harmony is projected by means of the fragrances and aromas coming out the kitchen. The mood of the house and the conversation that takes place therein are imbued with an aura of joy and happiness.

The ingredients for every recipe must be of the highest quality, taking note of proper food combining and choosing what is pleasing to the palate, in line with what is nutritionally required and the season of the year.

Learning to cook is high art. Each dish is a canvas where the ingredients provide the colors and our personal creativity provides the intention. To learn to cook, or practice one's talent if one already has the ability, means to follow the creative imagination and give way to artistic expression. Even the simplest of meals, with a dose of intelligent creativity, can become a work of art, pleasing to both sight and taste.

Once we have placed our dish on the table, we can offer our humble artwork to the spiritual presence that has inspired us on this particular day. And if you don't feel like doing this, but are only interested in the aphrodisiac potential of the meal produced, don't worry about it. Simply offer the meal to spirit, both your own and to the spirit of he, she, or they who are sharing the meal with you. Every heart is divine. Love is the important thing here. Love is the trademark of divinity. If you wish to honor the deities, do it in a heartfelt manner.

When you cook from your soul you imbue the food with your essence and thereby turn it into an extension of your spirit.

Feelings and Food

Do you know why your spiritual attitude and capacity to express joy are so important in the act of cooking? It's because everything is energy and there is a law of energy that teaches us "what you give you get back in return." This means that if we are sad we will provoke unhappiness in others, but if we are happy we will inspire joy in them. It is the quintessential "boomerang" effect.

Please read *Like Water for Chocolate*, by Laura Esquivel, where the main character is a cook who puts her lovesickness into everything she cooks. It is an ingenious, beautiful story and has science on its side.

We always tend to neglect the relationship between our emotions and the digestive process. When a person can't "stomach" a difficult situation, some rough patch or emotional upheaval in their life, it is certain they won't be able to properly digest their food and probably won't even have an appetite. Our desires are a

divine gift. They mean one is open, happy, and receptive to the banquet available to the senses.

Joyful eating is not something everyone enjoys. In 1998, when I visited Osho's Multiversity in Pune, India, I was struck by how the *sannyasins* (spiritual renunciants) ate. It was open air, under the mild noonday sun, with numerous tables filled with guests—an unforgettable spectacle. It wasn't the number of people that impressed me, it was how they enjoyed their food. Some ate in silence, attentive with every bite, others talked softly, laughing and enjoying, chewing with awareness and making their meal a meditation, and allowing its pleasure to permeate their entire being.

And this is what is most important: that we learn to experience the flavors and allow the body to take in food that is thoroughly masticated and mixed with the digestive enzymes of our saliva, accompanied with a right attitude.

A Matter of Health

Deepak Chopra, renowned doctor of Ayurvedic medicine, advises us to never eat when we are upset, or, even worse, to eat standing up. Those who eat in bars, the fast-food fans and *tapas* junkies, do not know what harm they do to their stomachs and digestion when they eat standing up and not sitting down comfortably at table.

In line with the principles of Chinese medicine, it is advised to never engage in quarrels or any type of heated discussion during lunch. According to this wise teaching, the heart meridian (one of the twelve principal meridians that conduct vital energy through the body) rules between the hours of 11 a.m. and 1 p.m. and later activates the meridian of the small intestine between the hours of 1 and 3 p.m.

Taking this into account, you can see how the anger-food-heart combination leads to nothing good.

According to both traditional Chinese medicine and Ayurveda there are five emotions detrimental to our organs: sadness (harms the lungs), boredom and ennui (the heart), worry (the spleen), anger (the liver), and fear (the bladder). The negative effects of these emotions are doubled if they are present while we eat. The surrounding emotions when we eat must be positive and turned toward mindfulness and contemplation of life, to joyful laughter, and conscious celebration.

This does not require you to lose track of your daily activities and busy schedule. To start off the day right we need a good boost of energy. It is said: "Breakfast like an Emperor, lunch as a King, snack as a pauper, and sup as a beggar." Nature provides laws of energy that we are bound to follow. Daytime is for action; nighttime is for rest. When the sun sets at dusk it is time to cease from general activities and relax. Anyone who wants to maintain their vital energy and live long (if it is their fate and the gods so will) must take care of their digestive mechanism.

To do this, you shouldn't eat when you are upset or overeat before you go to bed. Both have effects on our emotional state and digestion. It is quite probable we won't even remember our dreams (those soul messages most important for our growth) if we fail to follow this advice. Above all, remember that cooking is not just following a recipe. It involves a cycle of digestion, food combining, awareness, and enjoyment.

Food and Sexual Desire

In ancient cultures such as Greece and those of the Middle East and Far East (including India, Pakistan, Arabia, and Japan) it was a well-known fact that many foods possess aphrodisiac qualities that ignite sexual desire. Spices, roots, greens, and fruits such as ginseng, celery, seafood, cinnamon, and pepper, among others, have been used for centuries as natural stimulants of sexual passion.

Almost all the recipes I present in this book have an aphrodisiac character and can be used to activate the power of food pertaining to sexuality. Besides this, eating these foods will result in feeling more dynamic, fulfilled, energized, and ready to share the spice of love in the form of sex.

Both food and sex are vehicles of delight, the stuff of life. Food and body are both sacred and require care and attention. During the nine months of our gestation we are nourished by our mother's body. Our nutrition is divine, even from before the time we are born. Food sustains life, and during this period the body generates nutrients for both mother and the future baby.

The wise of yesteryear have bequeathed us combinations of foods to awaken our sexuality in a natural way and channel it for pleasure, and as vital sustenance for our survival and emotional health. If we bring our art to this, we are contributing in a way that maintains the flames of the fire of love.

Yin Foods, Yang Foods

In nature, everything is bipolar and consists of complementary opposites. The feminine and masculine energies bring about balance in all of life's manifestations. Summer/winter, day/night, sun/moon, man/woman, etc. It's the same with foods. There are foods that are energetically masculine and foods that are energetically feminine.

"Yin" and "Yang" are the polarities that generate life's current. Yin is cold, receptive, and subtle. Yang, on the other hand, is hot, acti-

ve, and generative. Traditional Chinese medicine emphasizes proper combining of these two principles to maintain health by way of right nutrition. Hippocrates said it thousands of years ago: "Let food be your medicine."

Usually, a woman needs Yin foods to activate her feminine nature (that which attracts her male counterpart) and, naturally, the man needs to consume Yang foods to enliven and boost his masculine energy (and so attract his female counterpart). The most important thing, however, is to properly combine foods with both energies.

For example, a woman should eat approximately 70 percent feminine (Yin) foods and 30 percent masculine (Yang) foods. The man should eat 70 percent masculine (Yang) and 30 percent feminine (Yin). This means the man should eat mostly meat, fish, or proteins such as soy and the woman vegetables, greens, and legumes, so that they both maintain their energetic attractiveness.

The energy a person emits is what attracts someone else to him or her. It can be sexual, spiritual, or even intellectual in nature. Attraction and repulsion proceed primarily from the interaction of the inner natures of the people concerned, but there are other factors to be considered such as body odor (certainly a function of what one eats), overall "vibe" of the people concerned, and body language.

Energy is vibration. The least we can do is choose the foods and combinations that further energetic congruence/harmony. The point of this is to keep the inner flame of heart, body, and mind burning brightly.

If one follows too limited a diet and represses natural cravings, it can result in the person losing vitality and the dimming of their inner light.

A balanced diet and regular exercise (yoga, Tantra, dance, Pilates, jogging, or whatever one prefers) will reinforce the complementary effects of nutrition, rest, and exercise.

Balanced Eating

Dieting is harmful to health since it implies restriction and prohibition. In contrast, to put ourselves in a balanced relationship with food allows us to grow and develop as persons. To ingest the necessary number of calories, to rest, to exercise, and to allow body and soul to be nourished with beautiful and uplifting things (painting, art, music, massage, food, sex, meditation . . .) will insure proper balance and elevation of our being.

Feminine Foods: olives, water, vegetables, fruit, milk, cheese, seaweed, tea, greens, rye, beets, oysters, yogurt, mint, almonds, butter, mussels, octopus, soy, etc.

Masculine Foods: fish, meat, eggs, radishes, garlic, onion, lentils, wheat, carrots, celery, apples, plantains, watercress, chicory, endive, salt, shrimp, lobster, corn flour, etc.

* Cereals contain equal amounts of Yin and Yang and are equally beneficial for men and women.

We shouldn't force restrictive diets on ourselves; we were born to enjoy and delight in all that is present before us. To eat intelligently means to dedicate the time necessary to prepare and love the foods we require. One must say NO! to junk food, any food that is processed and full of empty calories.

It is alarming how many obese people there are in the United States. This is due to two things: eating junk food, and a lack of self-esteem/self-love that results in an existential "hole" that people try to "patch over" with these foods. Hunger for love is something the soul seeks to satisfy, but it cannot be sated with food. Respect and love are the food required to fill this void. If you don't love yourself and others (the more the better, love expands with the giving), it is certain you will compensate by overeating.

Love and food are directly connected. When we love someone, we want to cook for them; the food is a symbol and manifestation of our feelings for them. Food should always be something we make to celebrate what we love, what we live for, what we dream of, and the fact that we are alive.

Cooking smart means preparing delicious meals, healthy and full of vitality, while keeping tab of the calories we consume and expend during the course of our day. If you exercise regularly and your glandular system is functioning properly there should be no reason to gain weight or give up on your body.

Food and Repression

When you eat, your mental/emotional state is very important since proper digestion depends on you being calm. Negative emotions, tension, haste, stress, and lack of enjoyment mean bad digestion, constipation, and other stomach problems.

If we eat attentively, offering our meal to the divinities, and we feel that what we are about to consume is tasty and nutritious (providing life and energy to our body), we will be feeding ourselves in the best possible way. Any form of repression is bad for us. It injures our psyche and results in unfulfilled yearning. The energy of such desires must go somewhere. Do you know where it goes?

Unfortunately, this energy gets trapped inside us, with no way out. It is not released. It is not expressed. To be expressed means its pressure is released. Repression, on the other hand, means the energy is maintained "under pressure." Repressing it means you generate this undesirable pressure within yourself, and living with this pressure it is unlikely that we can love, feel deeply, create, dream, dare. . . .

To eat without repression, knowing that we have purposely chosen foods that best suit us (though perhaps not always our favorites) we will feel satisfied and enjoy a state of inner well-being for our physical, mental, and emotional bodies.

Destruction, Creation, and Preservation

Shiva, Brahma, and Vishnu are the Hindu gods which represent the trinity of destruction, creation, and preservation that play out in all of life. These three corners of the triangle are intertwined with human evolution.

Example: One relationship ends (is destroyed) after a certain amount of time. Later, another one comes our way (is created) and we do everything we can to keep (preserve) it. The phrase "I'll always love you" refers to our desire to preserve something, to make the happiness we feel last forever.

Get rid of (destroy) your bad eating habits, heavy foods, fried foods, greasy foods, processed foods, etc. Create a new concept of eating based on healthy foods, light meals, good eating habits intelligently scheduled (eat a light meal every three hours), chewing thoroughly, eating in tranquil and pleasant surroundings. Finally, maintain (preserve) your inner glow with right eating, positive emotions, and a spiritual attitude.

If you ever wish to consider where your life is going, you need only examine what you need to let go and what you need to keep. This includes clothing, memories, habits, thoughts, eating habits, etc.

To let go of (destroy) harmful foods, you must create a new and intelligent way of eating and preserve your attitude of aware maintenance and personal care.

Processing Your Food as Well as Your Relationships

Negative emotions result in poor digestion. If you are someone who simply swallows without chewing well and tasting what you are eating it makes it even worse.

My father would tell me you have to "chew on" an idea before you take action on it. "To chew" means "to process." Life is something to be savored, chewed on, worked out. With cooking, eating, and experiencing reverence for our lives and the divinities, we enter a new frequency of living where pleasure motivates us and happiness and satisfaction flow naturally.

Pleasure is the language of the gods and those humans who dare to contact their own inner divinity. Equal in importance is learning to chew thoroughly, to close your eyes, experience the flavors, and enjoy every mouthful. Apply this to your personal relationships also: chew thoroughly any bad memories (so that you dissolve them), digest/process the negative emotions that knot your stomach and you will experience greater freedom with each new day.

Are We What We Eat, or What We Digest?

Proper nutrition can be cancelled out by bad digestion. To eat healthily does not mean just to pick the foods we think are right for our body. It is possible, for example, you are eating almonds but you are allergic to them or have some form of unconscious issue with them or they are not suited to your digestive system. Clearly, it is not what we eat, but what we *digest* that forms us.

Digestion is a process of assimilating and transforming the active ingredients of food in order to nourish our cells, muscles, bones, organs, and different bodily systems. Remember that the engine of your body is always active. Imagine your car's engine running continually, day and night. What would happen if you never turned it off, if you never let it rest? Clearly it would fail, it would seize, it would burn out completely. Accordingly, it is a good idea to give your body a rest and undertake a cleansing fast from time to time.

Good digestion depends on tranquility when you eat and proper food combining. I also advise that you process old emotional wounds that perhaps are unconscious and negatively affect various organs such as the stomach, liver, and intestines.

Many illnesses result from failure to process old angers and conflicts, pains, and suffering. Make *love* the food that nourishes your spiritual evolution and dissolves these negativities.

Make it your aim to forgive and absolve any conflicts you might have with those near to you with whom you don't get along, with a friend who hurt you, with a partner who wasn't on the up-and-up, with an ex-lover who caused you suffering (make sure to remember  the times you shared ecstasy) and free yourself from the energy blockage.

Well-digested food and assimilated emotional issues are vital to our sense of being light, free, liberated, and without conflict. It is the only way to really live. To forgive, to process past issues and start fresh greatly benefits us. There is no point in maintaining inner struggles and clouding the horizon of our life with them. All that does is deaden us, just as if we were to go to sleep after consuming an enormous meal.

Foods That Awaken Sexuality

Sex and food both nourish a human being. The need to eat and requirement for affection and bodily stimulation are equally worthy of satisfaction. I have given a number of Tantric techniques in my books: **El arte de tantra, Lecciones de sexo tántrico y Tantra, el sexo sentido,** that offer ways to bring sexual relations to an enormously more profound, pleasant, and aware level. These also raise the level of consciousness and bonding between lovers.

Tantra is a synthesis that envisions the possibility of an individual's supreme realization. It includes many modalities: philosophical, artistic, psychological, scientific, yogic, meditative, sexual, and nutritional. The latter two are the subject of this book.

It is known that nutrition affects the psyche, body, and emotions. More fundamental, however, is the power it has to either increase or decrease sexual energy. Certain foods reinforce the body's "octave of attraction" that not only generates the personal magnetism that attracts others, but also attracts the events of one's personal life.

Many people are unaware that the success of any enterprise, be it artistic, entrepreneurial, or personal, depends on whether or not one has this sexual and intellectual magnetism. Sexual energy is gold, the element that results from transmuting our animal instincts into divine awareness. By means of this transformed energy and the opening of awareness, we are able to create and shape our destinies, as an artist creates his or her art.

The Greeks, for example, saw the relationship of sexuality, celebration, and sustenance. This was above all the case with commemorations of Dionysus, god of pleasure, enjoyment, and wine.

As it is with food, so is it also with sex. Enjoyment is the nectar that feeds our inner divinity. It is a balm for both stress and worries. I always direct my students to comply with this saying attributed to Shakespeare: "No moment of our existence should pass without some pleasure." Pleasure and awareness are a formula for life that can bring us to personal happiness.

From top to bottom and left to right: seafood, ginkgo biloba leaf, oats, popcorn, cinnamon, celery, damiana herb, ginseng, and honey. All are powerful aphrodisiacs with quite different effects. For example, oats provide stamina for the male and, on the other hand, ginseng offers more subtle effects for both women and men.

Foods which positively enhance sexual function are many and varied: spices, greens, condiments. . . . The most effective are chocolate, cinnamon, celery, garlic, seafood, and chili peppers. It doesn't hurt to add some musk perfume to the mix for a ritual where food and sex share equal billing!

Rituals for The Beloved

Rituals remind us we are standing on sacred ground. Holiness is a matter of attitude. It has nothing to do with physical places; you don't have to go to a church or mosque to experience the holy. Your own home is your temple. And your heart is a treasure house of luminous creative energy you can share with others.

I love to create these rituals and use them for enchantment. A woman will fall into your arms, ecstatic, if you dedicate a supper to her goddess or any other divinity you choose to commemorate.

Rituals have power. A person, couple, or group of companions can join the energy of their thought, their *intention* and, using the power of a common meal, visualize an outcome they wish to bring into reality. It is this magic we have lost, a practice other cultures of the past respected and cultivated. We have lost veneration of the gods and natural forces. To recover the spirit of conscious, sacred

celebration, we must raise the level of our life spiritually and materially.

The goal of each life is glory, the realization of the destiny and use of the gifts that the infinite intelligence has given us to manifest. Let us consider, then, how a sacred meal can serve as a way to awaken the power that resides in each of us.

Step 1. Light Candles

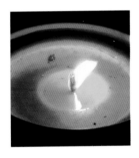

Candles, besides being a beautiful decoration, provide the element of fire. Fire is a magical element that tends upward. Its hypnotic flames warm and inspire our heart. A fiery heart is a living heart, full of enthusiasm and personal exuberance. People with fire in their blood are different from others. There is a light about them, an enchantment, a bright aura that always accompanies them.

When you light candles you have an opportunity to focus your personal intention. You can use this fire, this light, to ignite the process of bringing whatever you wish into form. You can silently ask for divine help in manifesting your desire. Your prayer will be heard—don't doubt this for a second—for the divinity is within you!

Light candles and take the time to offer them with your sacred intention. If your desire is to manifest a relationship, a project, or any situation that seems to be going nowhere or even appears to have gone up in smoke, use this ritual to turn on your inner power. Feel how the light surrounds you and bring this radiance to the meal you are about to prepare. This ritual is a way to show love and to bond with fellow travelers on that road where our destinies meet.

Step 2. Pour Yourself a Cup of Wine

Wine is the drink of the gods. Wine is the fruit of the vine. And the vine represents our earthly life. Wine is the drink that makes your soul shine.

Wine introduces celebration, euphoria, and power, along with the recognition that life is not just a matter of using our common sense, reason, logic, but is a surprising and ever-changing wonder that draws our spirit toward the heavenly realm.

But you must know your limit. If you go too far, you will end up on your butt, insensate, and out of it. One must use the "keys to the kingdom" wisely. Too much wine, like all excess, confuses that very vision we need for creating. As my father would always say: "Less is more!"

A cup is an empty vessel that we fill with the nectar of the grapes, along with the elements that produced it: earth (the Mother), sun (the Father), wind (the Spirit), and water (the Sustainer).

There is much magic in a bottle of wine. A beautiful journey entails from vine to lips: sure, certain, and deliberate. Dionysus is in every vine, in every sip.

A cup of wine can open the doors to the magical, to adventure, to hope, and to joy. Its powers enable you to walk the path of vision the gods have set before you. The gods  have created this game called "life" so that we might revel, and not struggle in it. Wine is a gift to enjoy and delight in.

Our difficulty lies in not understanding that the language of life is pleasure. Let every sip show you that you are a being of light and potential. It is said Jesus ate and drank wine at His final supper. The Church uses wine in Its ritual to represent the blood of Christ. Why is wine and a meal used to celebrate and commemorate a gathering?

Wine and food have always been part of feasts and celebrations. Let your cup of wine be filled with magic and life. I like to drink my wine in cups I bought on a trip to Greece. You can use whatever cup you like and make it your own soul ritual.

Remember that the path to equanimity is evoked by the concept of seeing the cup as half empty or half full.

In his magnificent book *The Prophet*, Kahlil Gibran says:

"And in the autumn, when you gather the grapes of your vineyards for the winepress, say in your heart: I too am a vineyard, and my fruit shall be gathered for the winepress, and like new wine I shall be kept in eternal vessels. And in winter, when you draw the wine, let there be in your heart a song for each cup; and let there be in the song a remembrance for the autumn days, and for the vineyard, and for the winepress."

Step 3. Put on Music

Music has tremendous power to wake up creativity and inspiration. I love to cook listening to my favorite artists, voices and melodies that wake up my soul: Greek *sirtaki* dancing, Demis Roussos, the Bee Gees, "chill out" music, or the Three Tenors. Whatever it is that you like, feel completely free to choose it. Music has always been the currency of stories and feelings. It is a curious fact that Karl Orff's opera *Carmina Burana* is a depiction of medieval monks gathering for a celebration of wine, women, and sensual pleasure and comes off as something erotic and seductive.

The authors of the ancient texts Orff used called themselves "the Goliards," i.e., Gluttons. They were errant religious students and clerics, portrayed in the Robin Hood tales as Friar Tuck.

These monks scorned the corruption of the clergy. They were bored with contemplative life and saw no sin in earthly life and temptations. Orff selected texts that represented the major themes of their poems: change, intoxication, irony, and sensual pleasures; things they totally embraced.

The music of the great masters fills us with stories of magic and life. Playing our favorite music as we cook, we "season" the meal with those feelings, affecting the food in the same way we have discovered music affects plants and the formation of ice crystals.

Step 4. Read Poetry

Honor your guest with a reading from your favorite text or poem. Gibran's *The Prophet* can be a great source of inspiration and enchantment. Who is not conquered by poetry, a cup of wine, intoxicating music, or a beautiful voice? What more do you need to manifest a magical, magnetic space? Choose what inspires you. May I suggest that you read Gibran, a genius who was able to convey deeply human sentiments using the fire and honey of words?

Here is what he says about self-knowledge:
"Your hearts know in silence the secrets of the days and the nights.
But your ears thirst for the sound of your heart's knowledge.
You would know in words that which you have always known in thought.
You would touch with your fingers the naked body of your dreams.
And it is well you should. The hidden well-spring of your soul must needs rise and run murmuring to the sea; And the treasure of your infinite depths would be revealed to your eyes.
But let there be no scales to weigh your unknown treasure.
And seek not the depths of your knowledge with staff or sounding line. For self is a sea boundless and measureless.
Say not, "I have found the truth," but rather, "I have found a truth." Say not, "I have found the path of the soul." Say rather, "I have met the soul walking upon my path." For the soul walks upon all paths. The soul walks not upon a line, neither does it grow like a reed. The soul unfolds itself, like a lotus of countless petals."

Step 5. Your Apron
A simple apron, besides protecting your clothes from stains, is the distinctive "tunic" worn by a chief.

In ancient times wise men of Greece, Egypt, Arabia, or India wore tunics. Why? The symbolism is worth noting.  Tunics and aprons are garments of one piece. They represent the body's unity. They are not like a shirt or pants that mark a division between higher and lower, superior and inferior. Who made this division? The Catholic Church!

Anything that generates division causes conflict. Many conflicts between instincts (lower zone), the desires of the heart (middle zone), and thought (top zone) have divided the human being into conflicting domains of action, feeling, and thinking.

When you don your apron of one piece, you assert the unity of your inimitable being, a divine oneness that manifests itself in the art of your cuisine.

Step 6. Choosing Your Ingredients
To go to the supermarket once a week means to choose ingredients for the recipes that you have decided to prepare. It's a good idea to

keep a pantry, making sure to maintain the freshness of its contents.

When you choose one of the recipes I offer for any of the gods or goddesses, the first step will be to gather the ingredients on the kitchen table and arrange them so they are conveniently at hand. Be aware of the principles of Feng Shui when you cook. Do everything by hand. Cook as if you were doing a walking meditation with a silent mind and awakened heart.

Cooking is a delight that allows you to explore the tastes and textures of ingredients as if they were colors on a palette for a painting you are about to create. Each dish fulfills the old saying: "The first bite is taken with the eyes." This goes not only for the actual cooking, but also applies to how the meal is presented.

Step 7. Sing When You Cook

To sing when you cook is one of the great pleasures of life and involves all of your senses. When you cook and sing, you energize your body, you perk up your ears, you stimulate your imagination, you wake up your taste with the different flavors, your fingers come alive to different textures, you invoke a sacred space, you commune with the divine presence, and you initiate a deep communion with the one with whom you will share the meal (eating solo is an expression of self-love that also has its own value). Lastly, and not least, to sing and cook means to enjoy the sensuality and magnetism of the meal itself.

To sing when you cook releases endorphins into the bloodstream, the so-called "pleasure endorphins." Sing from your heart and let your song go forth. You are cooking for gods and goddesses. . . . Music makes us dance, makes us feel, and makes us come alive. Life without music is unimaginable.

Step 8. Dress Up in Style

There is a saying: "Dress well, even when you beg." Elegance is a key that opens doors. Allow your clothes to decorate your natural beauty and to complement the garb of your spirit, your aura, and self-esteem.

Choose clothing that makes you feel good. Don't wait till Christmas to wear something that makes you look handsome or pretty. Dress to honor your inner divinity. Dress to please yourself first and to worship your inner being, and then for others and sharing divinity with them. Let your light shine, elegantly. Don't hide your divine spark under a bushel.

Step 9. Make a Meal that Surprises Your Lover

"What's up with you?" "Are you OK?" "It looks like someone hijacked my husband (boyfriend, girlfriend)!" These are some of the things your lover might say when faced with an unexpected dish if they are not accustomed to you popping culinary surprises on them.

To cook for the ones we love is a statement of feeling, caring, and kindness. Another day this could take the form of a massage or relaxing bubble bath. All of these provide a creative venue that can inspire love and personal caring between you and your partner or friends.

When you put all your talent, creativity, and magic into a special, romantic evening you create moments that become engraved in your soul.

Cooking Up Love in the Kitchen

A couple's sustenance requires attention, novelty, bonding, joy, and friendship. But there is also an aspect of sharing involved in the energetic requirements of generating

attraction (remember, what is inside us will either attract or repel others).

Along these lines, the aphrodisiac and healthy recipes that I have personally designed are intended to support our positive vibrations.

You can tell, immediately upon entering a home, the unique quality of its vibrations and if it has that special "at home" vibe. If the kitchen is cold and there's nothing in the fridge, or there is no pantry to keep ingredients, no greens or even canned goods, it will be a house but not a home. A kitchen offers intimacy and protection like no other room in the house. It is important to observe the principles of Feng Shui in our kitchens. Ingredients, utensils, provisions, and even lighting are a part of this. It must be an inviting place, a place where the passion of the smithy (cook) forges swords (the meal) of wisdom, intimacy, awareness, and celebration.

Cooking is an important part of the life of a couple. It gives both the opportunity to take turns surprising and gifting each other with sacred nutrition. If you live alone, cook what most appeals to you, and when you have guests, don't be afraid to show your cooking "chops."

Cooking and the Chakras

Within the scheme of the human energy system the *chakras* mark the basic energy points related to our survival: sex, food, and love. They are located, respectively, in the genital area (below the navel), pit of the stomach, and center of the chest.

Correct functioning of these centers balances us. There are three more chakras: one in the throat area (creativity), one in the middle of the forehead (intuition), and one at the top/crown of the head (spiritual).

When a chakra and the desire that corresponds to it are not satisfied, its energy is almost always diverted to the center responsible for regulating appetite and we end up overeating due to the resultant anxiety or stress. It is also possible for the opposite to happen, due to an emotional or sexual problem, and we can lose our appetite.

To avoid these kinds of problems I will offer you some tips on yogic cooking that will help you keep the chakras in alignment and maintain balanced nutrition, without it involving any strain.

anything for which we need to allot sufficient time it is eating with tranquility.

If you work for eight hours and sleep for eight hours that leaves you another eight for other tasks. It shouldn't take you more than forty-five minutes to cook a meal. To save time I suggest you cook with a plan, moving gracefully with focus and paying attention to the sequence of steps involved in the meal, washing the utensils as you go so that the kitchen is clean when you finish. Believe me, it is simply a matter of prioritizing and focus. It is possible to turn the simple act of cooking into an artistic expression that connects us with our body, other people, the gods, and enhances our communion with life.

Always cook with a festal attitude and not as a duty or obligation. If you are tired or out of sorts, it is better that you eat fruit or yogurt and not cook in a negative state. If you have fun when you cook and do it with music and wine, you will turn it into the perfect anti-stress therapy and a healthy diversion.

Cooking for People on the Go

Perhaps you're one of those who say: "I never have enough time for anything." But if there's

Yogic Wisdom for Eating

1. When you eat, be aware that food is a manifestation of Cosmic Consciousness and that you are using it to maintain your body (proving ground of your sexuality), as well as to keep your emotional and psychological health and satisfy the needs of your spiritual development.

2. Eat only when you are calm. Emotions influence your bodily state and digestion is disrupted by tensions, anger, and negativity. Sit comfortably, don't stand, so that you can relax and allow good digestion. Remember, we are what we *digest*, not just what we eat!

3. Eat three regular meals per day (breakfast, lunch, and dinner) and avoid in-between-meal snacks. The digestive system, in contrast to the heart, needs time to recuperate. Eating between meals can cause obesity, constipation, and lack of energy.

4. Chew your food thoroughly. This breaks down the food and mixes it with saliva, thereby facilitating enzymatic activity and the digestive process.

5. Make sure to eat a sufficient amount of fresh, raw foods. Avoid foods that are overcooked or overly-processed.

6. Drink plenty of water between meals, but not during meals. Sufficient water intake insures rapid elimination of waste, proper regulation of body temperature, and good digestion.

7. Avoid swallowing air with your food when you eat as this causes irritation of the stomach.

Greek Recipes

Light Aphrodisiac Suppers

About 2 pounds (1 kg) of prawns
1 cup of olive oil
Salt
1 clove of garlic
parsley
2 avocados
Some red quince
Some soft *Queso Fresco*
1 head of lettuce
pepper
2 lemons

Skin and Fire
Prawn Salad with Avocado and Quince

1. Season the prawns with a bit of olive oil, salt, finely chopped garlic, and parsley. Cut up the prawns, reserving some whole for garnishing.
2. Peel the avocados and dice them. Finely dice the quince and the *queso fresco*. Then mix the avocados, quince, and *queso fresco* together with the cut-up prawns. Mix well.
3. In the bottom of a salad bowl, toss the mix and place the whole prawns on top for display.
4. Spread fresh, finely cut lettuce on top and dress with plenty of pepper and lemon.

About 2 pounds (1 kg) of mussels
3 tomatoes
1 large onion
1 clove of garlic
1 cup of olive oil
Salt, pepper, and paprika

Aphrodite Hot
Spicy Mussels with Tomato Salsa

1. Wash the mussels, scrape off and discard the beards. Place the mussels in a pot with very little water and heat until they open. Take them off the stove and let cool. Meanwhile, prepare the salsa.
2. Grate the tomatoes and fry them in a pan for about fifteen minutes.
3. In a separate pan, sauté the onion (chopped) along with the clove of garlic (also chopped) in a little bit of olive oil until lightly golden in color. Then add salt, pepper, paprika, and finally the tomato salsa.
4. Lightly stir-fry the onion/garlic/tomato mix once over easy and remove from the fire. Empty this mix over the mussels, allowing the mollusks to thoroughly absorb the juice.

About 2 pounds (1 kg) mussels
3 peppers
1 cup of brown rice
1 onion
1 cup of olive oil
3 tomatoes
Salt, pepper, and seasoning.
2 green apples
2 cups of white wine

Steamed Mussels with Lemon, Apples, and Stuffed Peppers

1. Wash the mussels, scrape off and discard the beards. Place the mussels in a pot with very little water and heat them until they open. Take them off the stove and let them cool. In the meantime, prepare the filling for the peppers.
2. Wash the peppers. Cut off the top (so as to form a lid), remove the seeds, and put peppers (lid and bottom part) in an oven at low temperature for 10 minutes. Boil the brown rice for 25 minutes
3. Fry the onion (well diced) at medium flame in olive oil. Once it is golden in color, grate the tomatoes and sauté them. Add salt, pepper, and season to taste. Remove from the fire.
4. Stir the salsa mix into the drained, boiled rice, allow it to cool a while, and then stuff the peppers. Put the stuffed peppers in the oven until they turn golden in color.
5. Finely grate the green apples and soak in a bowl with the white wine. Put the grated green apples/wine mix on the mussels. Serve.

1 tin of cockles (saltwater clams)
2 tablespoons of lemon juice
½ teaspoon of ground white pepper
Mayonnaise
4 pieces of sliced bread

The Inevitable Attraction of Opposites

Canapés à la Aphrodite with Cockles

Cockles are one of the most aphrodisiac of mollusks. These canapés are easy and quick to make and provide an excellent hors d'oeuvres for an erotic menu.

1. Drain the cockles and mash them with the lemon juice and ground white pepper. Next, mix in mayonnaise.
2. Remove the peel from the bread slices and cut the slices in half, forming two triangles. Spread with the cockles salad and keep the canapés in the fridge for one (1) hour.

Canapés à la Aphrodite with Cockles

Grilled Fish with Caramelized Onions in Honey

1 sea bass or sole
1 pound (500 g) of prawns
1 hake
2 medium zucchini
2 green apples
14 plums
1 red pepper
1 green pepper
Salt, pepper, spices, and parsley
1 lemon

Grilled Fish with Caramelized Onions in Honey

1. Cut up the different fish (sea bass or sole, prawns, and hake) into fine cubes. Likewise, dice the zucchini, green apples, plums, and peppers (red & green).
2. Mix the vegetables and fruit with the fish and season with salt, pepper, parsley and spices. Sprinkle with lemon.
3. Put the pieces of fish and vegetables on skewers. Mix them up.
4. Put a few drops of oil on the cooking surface (griddle, grill, barbecue). Cook until brown on both sides and serve hot.

1 octopus of about 2 pounds (1 kg)
Pepper and oregano (or paprika)
2 cloves of garlic
2 cups of red wine
1 teaspoon of honey
2 small tomatoes

Hands of Honey

Roast Octopus with Tomato and Wine

1. Wash the octopus and boil it on a medium flame. As it cooks, add more water if necessary, making sure the octopus is sufficiently tender before you remove it. Cut the octopus into pieces.
2. Add together the pepper, oregano or paprika, diced garlic, wine, honey, and diced tomatoes. Toss these ingredients and then add to the cut-up octopus.

2 oranges
1 teaspoon of basil
4 tablespoons of olive oil
5 ounces (150 kg) of brie cheese

Intimate Union

Aromatic Cheese and Orange Snacks

1. Peel the oranges. Try to remove all the white part of the rind. Cut the oranges in slices about ½ inch (1 cm) thick and let them marinade in a mixture of the basil and olive oil for an hour.
2. Cut the brie so that you have one piece of cheese for each piece of orange and put both pieces on wooden toothpicks/small skewers.

Celery and Cauliflower Soup

56

Luminous Greek Lunches, Snacks, and Hors d'Oeuvres

Sudden Illumination

A Celery Soup to Awaken Desire

1 onion
4 ounces (100 g) of celery
1 cup of vegetable broth
3 tablespoons of butter
4 tablespoons of flour
Salt and paprika to taste
1 cup of milk

1. Peel the onion and chop it finely. Boil the onion and celery together in vegetable broth over a slow fire.
2. Meanwhile, melt the butter in a frying pan at medium heat and stir in the flour gradually. Keep stirring and add salt and paprika to taste.
3. Add this mix and the milk to the vegetable broth. Let it simmer 10 minutes, stirring occasionally.

Sensory Delight

Lover's Soup Spiked with Cinnamon

1 onion
1 pound (500 g) of pumpkin
About 1 cup (250 ml) of water
1 cup of apple juice
A pinch of marjoram and salt
1 tablespoon of milk
1 tablespoon of olive oil
A pinch of cinnamon

1. Peel the onion and mince it finely. Peel the pumpkin and dice it. Sauté the onion and pumpkin together in a pot.
2. Add the water, apple juice, and salt to taste. When the pumpkin is soft, add the milk. Put the pumpkin/milk mix in a blender; blend and then return to the pot to continue simmering. Before serving, dust with marjoram and cinnamon.

2 tablespoons of whipped cream
2 ounces (50 g) Apollo's Spread
  (Taramosalata)
4 slices of smoked salmon
1 zucchini
Black pepper
4 ounces (100 g) of watercress

Pink Passion

Smoked Salmon with Apollo's Spread (Taramosalata)

Apollo's Spread, i.e. Taramosalata, is a Greek-style caviar spread made with carp roe, potato mash, onion, lemon juice, and parsley. (You can buy it in any store that sells Greek food/products and in many supermarkets.) It is a blended spread and a wonderful complement to many fish dishes and has a gentle, aphrodisiac effect.

1. Mix the whipped cream with Apollo's Spread (Taramosalata) and spread it on the salmon slices. Wash the zucchini and cut into very thin slices. Place the slices of zucchini on the salmon and add black pepper to taste.
2. Put the salmon on a small heap of the watercress.

1 tablespoon of butter
2 ounces of mushrooms
1 chopped onion
2 fillets of sole
Salt, to taste
Juice of ½ lemon
1 cup Cava (sparkling white wine)
2 tablespoons of heavy cream
1 tablespoon of cognac
2 egg yolks
A dash of chopped parsley

Kiss of Fire

Sole Fillets with Cava (Sparkling White Wine)

1. First, melt the butter in a frying pan and add the mushrooms and onions. Sauté them for about 5 minutes.
2. Next, remove the mushrooms from the pan and keep them apart. Add the sole, salt, lemon juice, and Cava to the pan juice.
3. Cook slowly, covered, and when the fish is done, remove it from the pan and keep aside.
4. Beat the heavy cream, cognac, and egg yolks together and incorporate them into the sauce in the pan. Allow this to heat for a couple of minutes.
5. Place the sole on serving plates. Cover it with the sauce from the pan and garnish with the mushrooms and parsley.

Smoked Salmon with Apollo's Spread (Taramosalata)

1 cup of milk
4 ounces of Roquefort cheese
1 clove of garlic, chopped finely
4 pieces of toasted, sliced bread

A Tasty Souvenir

Roquefort Cheese with Garlic on Toast

1. Heat the milk in a saucepan. Just before it comes to a boil, add the Roquefort cheese and the finely-chopped garlic. Cook until it thickens to the desired consistency and spread on the toast.

About ½ pound (200 g) of goat cheese
About 1/3 pound (150 g) of Piquillo peppers
3 tablespoons of olive oil
1 tablespoon of finely chopped parsley
Small pieces of toasted bread

View from the Summit

Goat Cheese and Piquillo Pepper Canapés

1. First crumble the goat cheese and finely chop the Piquillo peppers. Mix together the cheese, peppers, olive oil, and parsley. Spread the mix on the toasted pieces of bread.

8 dates
4 ounces of goat cheese

The Inner Artist

Apollo's Dessert

The goat is one of the favored animals of Apollo.

1. Hollow the dates and stuff them with the goat cheese. If you wish, you can put the stuffed dates in the oven for a few minutes at medium heat.

Roquefort Cheese with Garlic on Toast

Prawns with Ginger Sauce

Savory, Spicy Dishes

4 large prawns
2 onions
1 piece of ginger root
1 tablespoon of sherry wine
1 tablespoon of ginseng syrup
1 tablespoon of soy sauce
Salt and pepper, to taste

Erotic Encounter
Prawns with Ginger Sauce

The poet Asclepiades of Samos noted: "For supper with one's lover there is nothing better than the aphrodisiac properties of prawns."

1. To prepare this dish, first boil all the ingredients together except the prawns. After 5 minutes, shell and de-vein the prawns and then add them to the mixture. Season and continue to cook for 5 minutes on a low flame.

14 ounces (400 g) of prawns
1 can of beer
1 clove of garlic
1 laurel leaf, cut up
1 pinch celery salt
1 pinch black pepper
2 tablespoons of chopped parsley
1 teaspoon of powdered English
   mustard
2 tablespoons of lemon juice
¼ teaspoon of ginger
¼ teaspoon of paprika

The Breath of Life
Prawns in Beer

1. Put all the ingredients, except the prawns, in a pot to simmer.
2. Clean the prawns well, but don't remove the shells, and add them to the concoction. Boil exactly 3 minutes and drain. Serve the prawns with well-chilled white wine.

30-40 clams
Unsalted butter

Aphrodisiac Clams

Here is a simple, powerful recipe for waking up the libido and *kundalini* (psycho-sexual energy). The aphrodisiac properties of clams have been known for millennia.

1. Use fresh-caught clams. To know if they are fresh, trust your nose. Reject those whose smell isn't fresh and clean (you should smell the sea). Keep them in cold water for 20 minutes, then clean them thoroughly (wear rubber gloves to protect your hands) with a brush.
2. Cook the clams in boiling water and when they have opened up totally, remove them and let them drain. Put the clams in a serving bowl and put the clam broth and butter in separate containers. To maximize the aphrodisiac effect of this delicacy, dip the clams in their broth and dab with butter.

1 ripe mango
14 ounces (400 g) of cooked
   lobster
8 cooked prawns
4 ounces (100 g) of red-leaf lettuce
4 ounces (100 g) of mâche greens
   (Valerianella locusta)
3 tablespoons walnut oil
1 tablespoon raspberry vinegar

Constant Companionship
Lobster and Mango Salad

The mango is one of the most venerated fruits in India as an aphrodisiac food, and if combined with lobster it guarantees a night of passion!

1. Peel the mango and cut it into $3/8$" (1 cm) cubes. Shell the lobster and prawns, and cut the lobster into slices.
2. Place the lettuce and mâche greens on a serving plate and bathe them with the vinaigrette of walnut oil and raspberry vinegar. Place the lobster, prawns, and mango cubes on top of the salad.

Lobster and Mango Salad

2 pounds (1 kg) morello (sour) cherries
1 pound (500 g) of sugar
2 cups of cognac
2 teaspoons of cinnamon
Grated ginger
4 clove buds

Water and Feelings

Ginger Energy Drink

1. Wash and drain the morello cherries and put them with the sugar in a hermetically sealed (tightly sealed) jar. Let this sit for a month in the sunlight.
2. After the month is up, open the jar and add the cognac, cinnamon, ginger, and cloves. Reseal the jar and let it sit another 20 days.
3. Strain the liquor and bottle it. You will be surprised how much energy is contained in just one sip!

4 artichokes
3 carrots chopped in big pieces
4 potatoes cut in large chunks
3 scallions cut in large pieces
1–2 cups of oil
Juice of 3 lemons
1 tablespoon of flour
Salt and pepper

Evening Storms

Artichokes with Vegetables

1. Wash the artichokes and remove the tough, outer petals. Cut off the top of the artichokes with a knife. Remove the hearts. Put the artichokes in water and add half of the lemon juice so they don't oxidize.
2. Sauté the vegetables in oil for a few minutes and then add the artichokes, salt, and pepper.
3. Mix the remaining half of the lemon juice with water and the flour and pour over the sautéed vegetables. Make sure the mix is covered with water.
4. Cover the pot and simmer slowly for approximately 1 hour. Serve either hot or cold.

Virgin olive oil

3 zucchinis cut in fine slices (rounds)

3 medium onions chopped finely

1 clove of garlic chopped finely

1 pound ground lamb (or substitute an equal amount of tofu)

½ pound (250 g) of canned tomatoes

4 ounces (125 g) of tomato puree

1 tablespoon of oregano, dried or fresh (chopped)

½ cup of red wine

¼ cup of chicken or vegetable broth (optional)

1 tablespoon of salt (optional)

Black pepper, to taste

½ pound peeled, roasted potatoes, cut into thin slices

Butter (to rub on the pan)

1 ounce (25 g) of Parmesan cheese (to sprinkle on top)

To prepare the béchamel sauce:

1 ounce (30 g) of butter

1 tablespoon of all-purpose white flour

Milk

Yogurt

Rain of Passions

Zucchini Moussaka

1. Heat the oil on a medium flame and fry the zucchini slices on both sides for 3 minutes. Remove from the oil with a skimmer and place the slices on absorbent paper towels.

2. In the same frying pan, gently brown the onion and garlic until they are transparent. Add the ground lamb (or tofu) and let it cook for 5 minutes or so. Add the canned tomatoes with their juice, the tomato purée, oregano, red wine, broth, and seasoning. Lower the flame and let this cook for about 20 minutes or until the liquid is evaporated.

3. Turn on the oven. While the oven is warming, prepare the béchamel sauce. Slowly melt the butter in a small saucepan on medium high heat. When it is melted, add the flour and stir. Keep the flame low and keep stirring until it starts to thicken.

4. Add milk and keep stirring until you obtain a thick cream. After you reach the desired consistency, remove and season. Add yogurt to taste.

5. By this time, the lamb (or tofu) filling should be ready. Apply a light coating of oil to the inside of a baking tin (should be about 4 inches [10 cm] deep), and then put a layer of half the zucchini and potatoes on the bottom. Pour half of the filling over this, then add another layer of the zucchini/potatoes and then the rest of the lamb (or tofu) mixture. Cover this with the béchamel sauce and then, finally, dust the top with the Parmesan cheese. Bake for around 25 minutes, or until the top turns golden brown.

6. When done, remove from the oven and let it set a while. Serve hot.

Paella of Aphrodisiac Delights

4 tablespoons of olive oil
2 ounces (50 g) of chopped celery
1 tablespoon of chopped parsley
1 chopped green pepper
A pinch of paprika
3 cloves of chopped garlic
5 ounces (150 g) of sliced chicken breast
7 ounces (200 g) of rice
4 diced red tomatoes
1 teaspoon of saffron
Salt and pepper, to taste
1 dozen clams
1 dozen mussels
3 tablespoons of white wine
About 11 ounces (300 g) shelled prawns
2 cooked and shelled lobster tails
6 chopped artichoke hearts
4 ounces (100 g) of pitted green olives
4 ounces (100 g) of canned red peppers, chopped

4 fillets of fish (white flesh) without bones
¼ cup of self-rising flour
1 beaten egg
½ cup of white wine
3 cups of bread crumbs
¼ cup of olive oil

Paella of Aphrodisiac Delights

This paella is a veritable orgy of aphrodisiac ingredients and includes foods that are sure to wake up your libido (celery, saffron, paprika, clams, and mussels). If you and your partner are willing to take it on, I guarantee you will end up spending a night of unlimited passion!

1. Start by sautéing the celery, parsley, green pepper, paprika, and garlic in olive oil. Add the chicken breast and when it is golden, turn off the flame.
2. In a separate pot, boil the rice in 4 cups of water for 20 minutes with the diced tomatoes, saffron, salt and pepper to taste. In another saucepan, steam the clams and mussels (make sure to clean them beforehand) in a bit of water and when they open add the wine, prawns, lobster, artichoke hearts, olives, and chopped red peppers.
3. Mix everything together in an earthenware casserole and bake for 10 minutes at medium temperature and serve hot.

Erotic Encounter
Fried Fish au Vin Blanc

1. Cut the fish fillets in half lengthwise and remove all moisture by drying them on paper towels. In a small bowl, heap up the flour and make a hollow in the center, as if it were a small volcano.
2. Put the beaten egg in another bowl and add the white wine to it, stirring as you pour it in, then take the egg/wine mix and add it slowly to the hollow of the "volcano," stirring with a wooden spoon so that you form a smooth mixture without lumps. Put the bread crumbs on a separate plate.
3. Place the pieces of fish in the batter so that they are completely covered. Then remove and let the excess batter run off.
4. Press the battered fillets in the breadcrumbs, pressing them down so that a uniform coating is achieved on both sides. Put the olive oil in a frying pan and heat it at medium flame without letting it smoke. Fry the fish two at a time until they are golden on both sides.
5. Remove the fried fillets and set on paper toweling to absorb excess oil before you serve them.

Recipes for Ardent Lovers

3 tomatoes
1 small cucumber
1 medium onion
2 small green peppers
2 tablespoons of olive oil
Salt
Parsley and marjoram
4 ounces (100 g) of feta cheese
24 black olives

Wrapped in Your Hair
Greek Salad

1. Wash the tomatoes and quarter them. Peel the cucumber and cut it crosswise into slices. Wash the green peppers, cut off the tops, and remove the seeds. Cut into rings.
2. Mix all ingredients and put in individual bowls. Dress with the olive oil and add a pinch of salt.
3. Cut up the parsley and marjoram. Cut the feta cheese into cubes. Put the cheese and olives into the bowls and sprinkle the chopped parsley and marjoram on top. Serve.

1 cup of white wine
1 clove of chopped garlic
A pinch of thyme
1 tablespoon of chopped onion
2 tablespoons of butter
A pinch of salt
12 oysters
2 eggs

Sleight of Hand
Oysters and Eggs

1. In a saucepan, simmer the wine, garlic, thyme, onion, 1 tablespoon of butter, and salt for 6 minutes.
2. Detach the meat of the oysters from the shell and add to the saucepan. Cook another 2 minutes and remove from the fire.
3. Use the remainder of the butter to grease two tall molds and divide the mix between them. Add 1 egg to each mold, on top of the mix, and cook in a water bath around 10 minutes at 350° F (180° C). Serve this powerfully aphrodisiac dish warm and accompany with chilled white wine.

Desire

Greek Zucchini Cheese Pies

5 small zucchinis
1 chopped onion
2 fresh tomatoes
1 teaspoon of olive oil
2 sheets of fillo dough
5 ounces (150 g) of cottage cheese
Salt and pepper, to taste
Mix of grated nutmeg and 25
    chopped almonds
1 sprig of parsley
4 ounces (100 g) of butter
white or brown sugar, to taste

1. Set the oven to 450° F (230° C) for 15 minutes.
2. Cut the zucchinis into small, fine pieces, and sauté with the onion in a bit of olive oil. Add the tomatoes.
3. Spread one leaf of the fillo dough on the bottom of a mold that has been previously buttered. Add the zucchini mix, cottage cheese, salt, pepper, and mix of nutmeg and almonds. Butter the second fillo sheet and cover the pie.
4. Top with parsley and sprinkle a bit of white or brown sugar on top to sweeten the pie so it turns a nice golden color. Bake at 400° F (210° C) for 20 minutes.

Fiery Embrace

Chicken Curry with Ginger Vegetables

2 tablespoons of corn oil
4 chicken thighs
1 chopped onion
1 teaspoon of salt
1 clove of chopped garlic
1 teaspoon of powdered ginger
1 teaspoon of curry
1 chopped green pepper without
    seeds
2 tablespoons of boiled water
5 tablespoons of natural yogurt
Cooked rice
2 tablespoons of olive oil
1 chopped leek
2 tablespoons of butter

Curry and ginger will turn this dish into an authentic sexual rush.

1. Heat the corn oil in a frying pan and brown the chicken thighs. Next, using an electric blender, blend the onion, ½ teaspoon of salt, garlic, ginger, curry, green pepper, water (boiled), and yogurt. Once this is homogenized and creamy in consistency, pour it over the chicken in the frying pan and simmer for 30 minutes.
2. While the above is simmering and with around 12 minutes left until it's done, put rice in a frying pan with olive oil, the leek, and the rest of the salt and sauté.
3. After 15 minutes, remove the rice mix from the flame and let it sit covered for 5 minutes. To serve, mix the butter with the rice and serve it separately from the curried chicken.

2 pounds (1 kg) of crushed almonds

2 tablespoons of cinnamon

2 pounds (1 kg) of fillo dough

14 ounces (400 g) of whipped butter

Whole cloves

For the syrup:

2 pounds (1 kg) of sugar

4 cups of water

1 teaspoon Vanilla

Lemon juice

Baklava

1. Mix the crushed almonds with the cinnamon. Butter a baking pan and place a fillo leaf on the bottom. Brush melted butter on this leaf. Cover with another leaf and butter. Repeat for a total of three leaves on the bottom of the pan to start.

2. Spread some almond mix on the bottom leaves and cover with a sheet of buttered fillo. Repeat by spreading almond mix on this and, again, cover with a sheet of buttered fillo.

3. Continue with the above process until you have 4 sheets of fillo left. Butter these and place on top (don't cover with filling). Cut the baklava in its pan in the shape of little rhombuses (i.e. diamond-shaped). When you are done, stick a clove bud in each rhombus. Bake the baklava at medium temperature for an hour.

4. Prepare the syrup by dissolving the sugar in the water with the lemon juice. Let this simmer on a medium flame, adding the vanilla, until you obtain a syrupy consistency. Don't let it get too thick.

5. Remove the baklava from the oven when the top is golden. Let it cool down. Then pour the syrup over it. Let it sit until it is room temperature before you serve.

Baklava

Almond Chicken

2 chicken breasts
2 tablespoons of olive oil
½ teaspoon of saffron
1 cup of chicken broth
4 ounces (100 g) of long-grained
    rice
Salt
1 ounce (25 g) of shelled almonds
1 ounce (25 g) of shelled
    pistachios
1 onion
2 tablespoons of sugar
Grated rind of 1 orange
3 tablespoons of water

1 pound (450 g) of natural yogurt
½ cucumber
3 cloves of garlic, mashed
2 tablespoons of chopped mint
2 tablespoons of olive oil
1 tablespoon of vinegar
1 tablespoon of salt

2 egg yolks
½ lemon
1 teaspoon of salt
2 tablespoons of mayonnaise
2 tablespoons of natural yogurt
4 ounces (100 g) of caviar
1 teaspoon of Worcestershire sauce

Love's Play

Almond Chicken

1. Fry the chicken breast in olive oil and add the saffron and broth. Simmer over a low flame for 20 minutes. Separately, cook the rice in salted water for 20 minutes. Fry the almonds and pistachios and set aside. Fry the onion (chopped) until golden.
2. Prepare a thick caramel syrup by simmering the sugar and grated orange peel together in water.
3. Finally, strain the rice and put it on the serving plates. Place the chicken on top of the rice, then the nuts and onions on top of the chicken, then pour the caramel sauce on top of it all.

Side Dish

Tzatziki

1. Pour the yogurt in a medium container. Peel and grate the cucumber separately, removing excess water. Add to the yogurt. Then add the garlic, chopped mint, oil, vinegar, and salt.
2. Cover and refrigerate until you serve. Garnish with mint leaves.

Soul-Full

Caviar Stuffed Eggs

1. Use the old trick of rubbing the eggshell with the lemon half. This will prevent the egg from breaking when you boil it. It also will cause any cracks to mend.
2. Boil the eggs in salted water for 15 minutes. Then run cold water over them to cool them down. Remove the shells and cut the eggs in half, lengthwise.
3. Separately, mix the mayonnaise, yogurt, egg yolks (remove from the boiled eggs), caviar, and Worcestershire sauce. Stuff the hollows of the boiled eggs with this mix and put on plates to serve.

Prawns for an Erotic Appetite

Summer Bath

Prawns for an Erotic Appetite

2 tablespoons of olive oil
1 clove of chopped garlic
A pinch of paprika
11 ounces (300 g) of cooked and
    peeled prawns
4 tablespoons of mayonnaise
2 tablespoons of tomato sauce
½ teaspoon of lemon juice
1 tablespoon of chopped green
    olives
1 tablespoon of chopped parsley
1 chopped hard-boiled egg
Salt & pepper, to taste

1. Mix the olive oil, chopped garlic, and paprika in a bowl. Spread the mix over the prawns and let sit for an hour and a half.
2. Next prepare the sauce. Using a whisk, beat the mayonnaise, tomato sauce, lemon juice, chopped green olives, parsley, and chopped hard-boiled egg.
3. When the sauce is well homogenized, bathe the prawns in it and you are ready to enjoy!

A Surprise of Sparks

Lobster and Celery Appetizers

7 ounces (200 g) of cooked lobster
    (shelled)
Celery stalks
1 teaspoon of dill
4 ounces (100 g) of cream cheese
1 teaspoon of Tabasco sauce
2 tablespoons of mayonnaise
2 tablespoons of lemon juice
Salt & pepper, to taste

After making love, if you have the urge to continue, these celery and lobster appetizers will supply the necessary vigor to carry on!

1. Put all the ingredients, except the celery stalks and lobster, into an electric blender and blend until you get a homogenous filling. Fill the celery stalks with the mix and put in the refrigerator for ½ hour.
2. Serve the stuffed celery stalks with the cooked lobster and enjoy your energy re-supply!

20-30 mussels
3 cloves of chopped garlic
1 teaspoon of anise
½ teaspoon of oregano
1 tablespoon of chopped parsley
A pinch of hot chili pepper
3 red tomatoes skinned and cut up
1 cup of white wine
Salt and pepper, to taste
A Pinch of basil

Sea of Passion

Mussels to Die For

1. Clean the mussels well under a faucet of cold water using a brush. Wear rubber gloves so you don't cut yourself.
2. Put all the ingredients except the mussels, wine, and parsley, into a pot and simmer for 30 minutes. Then taste for salt & pepper, adjust as necessary, and add the wine and parsley.
3. Cover the mussels with water in a pot separately and simmer until they open. Drain them and then pour the sauce you have prepared over them.

4 fillets of sole
1 teaspoon of salt
½ teaspoon of dill
8 king prawn tails
2 tablespoons of flour
3 tablespoons of butter
4 tablespoons of olive oil
5 blossoms of saffron
1 cup (2 dl) of fish broth

Every Conch Has Its Pearl

Brochettes of Saffron Sole and King Prawns

1. Put the fillets of sole on your worktop and season with the salt and dill. Next, divide the prawn tails evenly between the fillets and roll the fillets around the prawns. Close the brochettes with small wooden skewers and dredge them in the flour.
2. Heat the butter and olive oil in a pan and fry the brochettes for 5 minutes. Grind the saffron blossoms separately.
3. Remove the brochettes from the frying pan and cook them in the fish broth for 10 minutes, adding the rest of the salt and the ground saffron blossoms.

Brochettes of Saffron Sole and King Prawns

½ pound (250 g) of red fruits (cherries, strawberries, raspberries)
Juice of 1 lemon
1 teaspoon of black pepper
½ teaspoon of white pepper
A pinch of cayenne
2 tablespoons of apple vinegar
1 pound (500 g) of cleaned anchovy fillets
4 tablespoons of olive oil
A pinch of salt

Bump & Grind

Anchovy Fillets Marinated in Fruit Juice

1. Whisk the fruit with the lemon juice, black and white pepper, and vinegar.
2. Next, put the anchovy fillets in the fruit marinade, cover with plastic wrap, and let them soak for 8 hours.
3. Lastly, remove the fillets, put them on serving plates and dress them with salt and oil.

1 tablespoon of butter
2 ounces (50 g) of mushrooms
1 chopped onion
2 fillets of sole
Salt, to taste
Juice of ½ lemon
1 cup white sparkling wine (or champagne)
2 tablespoons of cream
1 tablespoon of cognac
2 egg yolks
Some chopped parsley

A Glance and a Rose

Sole Fillets in White Sparkling Wine

1. Melt the butter in a frying pan and add the mushrooms and chopped onion. After 5 minutes, remove the mushrooms and set them aside.
2. Put the sole, salt, lemon juice, and sparkling wine in the frying pan with the onions. Cover and simmer. When the fish is done, remove it from the pan and set aside.
3. Beat the cream, cognac, and egg yolks together and add to the sauce. Let it heat together a couple of minutes.
4. Put the sole on serving plates, pour the sauce over it, and garnish with the mushrooms and parsley.

6 ounces (175 g) of prawns
3 tablespoons of olive oil
1 teaspoon of salt
1 pinch of cayenne pepper
½ cup of water
1 tablespoon of chopped mint leaves
7 ounces (200 g) of fava beans
1 tablespoon of unflavored gelatin powder

Sighs of Pleasure

Erotic Mousse of Prawns and Fava Beans

1. Peel the prawns and keep the shells and heads. Season the tails of the prawns with salt and cayenne pepper and fry them in olive oil for 2 minutes. Set them aside. In the same frying pan, add the water, the mint, the heads, and shells of the prawns. Cook for 5 minutes on a low flame.
2. Strain the mix from the frying pan and put the juice on the flame again. When it comes to a boil, add the fava beans and cook them till they're tender.
3. Turn off the heat and quickly add the gelatin powder. Remove and put the mix in a blender and blend. Into each mold pour the mix and add the prawn tails. In 2 hours the mousse will have set and this delicious plate will be ready to serve.

Mediterranean Delights

1 quart (1 l) water
1 teaspoon of salt
11 ounces (300 g) of fresh egg
   noodles
3 tablespoons of olive oil
7 ounces (200 g) of fresh salmon
Juice of 1 lemon
1 tablespoon of fresh mint leaves
   2 ounces (50 g) of black olives
   (pitted)
1 teaspoon of butter

Penetrating Intelligence
Fresh Egg Noodles with Black Olives and Salmon

1. Put the water in a pot, add salt, and bring to a boil. Throw in the egg noodles. Boil until done (about 15 minutes), remove and drain. Next, spread oil on the salmon and fry it for 5 minutes each side.
2. Remove the salmon. Using the same frying pan, put in the rest of the oil, the lemon juice, the mint leaves, and the olives. Crumble the salmon and put it in the frying pan with the butter. Fry for 5 minutes. Pour the contents of the frying pan over the egg noodles.

½ clove of garlic
4 tablespoons of dry white wine
1 pound (500 g) of gruyere cheese
A pinch of nutmeg
1 teaspoon of powdered mustard
3 tablespoons of kirsch (cherry
   brandy/liquor)
Salt & pepper, to taste
French bread cut into 1 inch (2
   cm) cubes

In the Shade of Your Bower
Fondue for Lovers

A cheese fondue is a wonderful dish to awaken passion, not only due to the aphrodisiac effect of the cheese, but also to sharing the meal out of one bowl. You can heat things up by dipping the sops of bread and putting them in your lover's mouth!

1. Rub the inside of the fondue pot with the half clove of garlic. Put the wine in first and when it is simmering, add the cheese, nutmeg, mustard, kirsch, salt, and pepper.
2. When the cheese is melted and the mixture is homogeneous, you are ready to bring it to table and dip the bread cubes.

10 grape leaves
3 chopped onions
Oil
Fresh mint leaves
9 ounces (250 g) boiled rice
Salt and pepper, to taste
Nutmeg, to taste
Cinnamon, to taste
3 ounces (80 g) pine nuts
5 ounces (150 g) raisins
Juice of 1 lemon

Wrapped in Skin

Grape Leaf Dolmades

1. Blanch the washed grape leaves for 15 minutes. Sauté the onion in oil and add the mint, rice, seasonings, pine nuts, and raisins.
2. Put some of the filling in each of the leaves at the bottom where the stem (previously trimmed) issues (shiny surface of the leaf faces downward), fold in the sides and roll to the tip, as if making a cigar.
3. Put the dolmas in a pot and add the lemon juice. Cover with water and put a plate on top of them to prevent them from unraveling. Cook for an hour on a low flame.

1 tablespoon of butter
1 tablespoon of brown sugar
1 tablespoon of cinnamon
Juice of ½ an orange
½ pound (250 g) of apricots
2 cups (500 ml) of red wine

Sweet Orgasms

Apricots with a Touch of Cinnamon

1. Skin the apricots, remove the pits, and cut them in half.
2. Put the butter in a pan and mix in the sugar, cinnamon, and orange juice until you obtain a homogenous syrup.
3. Add the apricots and sauté for a few minutes until they absorb the syrup. Add the red wine and serve this dessert while it is still warm in order to take advantage of its aphrodisiac-dionysian effects!

½ pound (250 g) of red peaches
½ pound of queso blanco or semi-hard goat cheese (feta)
4 ounces (100 g) of pitted, black olives
Orange liquor

Burning Desire

Peaches, Olives, and Cheese with Orange Liquor

1. Cut the peaches and cheese into slices.
2. Chop the olives finely and sprinkle them over the peaches and cheese. Add a drizzle of orange liquor.

2 chicken breasts cut into ⅜ inch (1 cm) cubes
2 ounces (50 g) of mushrooms
2 tomatoes
4 ounces (100 g) of pitted black olives
2 tablespoons of olive oil
2 tablespoons of butter
Salt
Pepper
1 tablespoon of flour
3 tablespoons of cognac
1 cup of red wine
2 truffles

Love and Dancing

Chicken with Olives Dredged in Cognac

This chicken with truffles is a stimulating aphrodisiac and an ideal precursor to a night of sensuality.

1. Fry the chicken along with the mushrooms (cut thinly), and the tomatoes (chopped), adding the pitted black olives and the butter. Season to taste and add the flour.
2. After 10 minutes, add the cognac and cook another 10 minutes at high temperature. Add the red wine and continue to cook for another 20 minutes. With 5 minutes left, add the truffles. Serve this dish with red wine.

2 ounces (50 g) of butter
4 ounces (100 g) of smoked
   salmon
1 tablespoon of heavy cream
4 eggs
4 ounces (100 g) of watercress

Leaping to the Glory of the Wise

Salmon with Eggs, Olives, and Watercress

1. Use the butter to grease two earthenware casseroles.
2. Cut the salmon in strips and divide them between the two casseroles. Divide the heavy cream and eggs between the two casseroles as well.
3. Put the earthenware casseroles in baking pans and add water to make a water bath for them. Cook until the eggs are done. Serve over watercress.

½ pound (250 g) of brie cheese
½ pound (250 g) of queso fresco
4 ounces (100 g) of pitted, black
   olives
Grated ginger
Honey

Eternally Youthful Skin

Cheese with Olives, Honey, and Ginger

This can serve as an appetizer for the other dishes.

1. Cut up the cheese into small pieces. Chop the black olives finely and sprinkle them on the cheese.
2. Add the grated ginger and honey, pouring them over the entire mix. To finish it off, you can sprinkle with a touch of oregano.

½ quart (½ l) of water
½ pound (250 g) of sugar
Juice of 1 lemon
5 oranges
1 bottle of sparkling wine or
  champagne
1 egg white

Sparkling Wine Sherbet

Sparkling wine helps fight shyness and disposes us to love. This sherbet is ideal to finish supper and start off a long night of passion.

1. Prepare the syrup: boil the water and add the sugar and lemon juice and stir until you obtain an even consistency.
2. Next, squeeze 4 oranges and peel the other, cutting its sections in half. Mix half of the sparkling wine with the syrup and the rest of the ingredients.
3. Put it all in a blender and add the rest of the wine. Blend, then put it in the freezer for 3 hours. Blend again, and let it re-freeze.

4 ripe figs
2 cups of Greek yogurt
1 tablespoon of honey
Some mint leaves

An Orgasm of Taste
Greek Yogurt, Figs, and Honey

1. Wash the figs well under lukewarm tap water and cut them in half. Place in the serving plates.
2. Mix the yogurt and honey and pour over the figs. Put in the refrigerator for at least two hours and garnish with the mint leaves just before serving.

1/2 tablespoon of cardamom
1 teaspoon of cinnamon
1 teaspoon of nettle seeds
1 slice of ginger root, cut up
1 demitasse of water
1 demitasse of honey
2 ripe peaches

Honey Breasts

Peaches in Cardamom and Cinnamon Syrup

1. Mix the cardamom, cinnamon, nettle seeds, and ginger with 2 tablespoons of water. Stir well. Next, add the rest of the water and put in a blender and blend the mix.
2. Boil the mix for 1 hour and add the honey. Peel the peaches and remove the pits. Cut them in half and bathe them in the cardamom and cinnamon syrup.

1 quart (1 liter) of water
4 tablespoons of powdered sugar
1 tablespoon of white wine
Juice of 1/2 lemon
3 passion fruit or papayas
3 peeled peaches
12 grapes

Dionysian Sorcery

Passion Dessert

1. Boil the water and add the sugar, making a light syrup. Remove from the heat and add the white wine and juice of the lemon. Put aside for a while.
2. Cut up the passion fruit (or papaya) and mash. Pass the pulp through a strainer.
3. Add the juice from the passion fruit/papaya to the syrup. Then add the peaches and mix well. Keep in the refrigerator for a minimum of 24 hours. Finally, serve in dishes or cups with the grapes as a garnish.

Dionysian Grapes

1 cup of Muscatel wine
2 tablespoons of cognac
2 cups (500 ml) of milk
1 cup of heavy cream
1 tablespoon of sugar
2 pinches of nutmeg

Passion Punch

For this punch to have its full effect, don't serve it too cold so that it can wake up your most sensual passions.

1. Mix all the ingredients except the nutmeg and pour into two cups.
2. Just before you serve, add a pinch of nutmeg to each cup.

2 cups (500 ml) of water
2 cups (500 ml) of orange juice
3 cups (750 ml) of sweet wine or Muscatel
2 tablespoons of sugar
A pinch of cinnamon
11 ounces (300 g) of melted dark chocolate
2 bunches of white or red grapes

Abundant Life with Orgasms to Boot!

Dionysian Grapes with Sweet Wine and Chocolate

1. Boil the water with the orange juice, wine, and sugar. Add the cinnamon. Let it simmer a while.
2. Gently heat the chocolate until it melts and is smooth and thick. Put the grapes in a bowl without separating them (you will have the chance to lick your fingers later).
3. Pour the wine and orange juice over the grapes and, finally, the melted chocolate over it all.

Power Breakfast

Hindu Recipes

Power Breakfasts and Light Meals

Energy for Dancing
Shiva's Breakfast

1 cup (¼ l) of soy milk
8 ounces (250 g) of breakfast
    cereal
2 peaches
A pinch of cinnamon
Honey

1. Put milk in a bowl. Add the cereal and mix well. Cut the peaches in small slices. Sprinkle with cinnamon and drizzle with 1 tablespoon of honey.

Jump Starting Your Enthusiasm
Power Breakfast

1 small slice of pineapple, peeled
    and cut up
1 sliced banana
2 rice cakes spread with queso
    fresco and honey
1 cup of Greek yogurt or kefir
1 small serving of brown rice
1 cup of green tea

This breakfast will give you all the energy you need to take on your day. Eat the fruit first so that it goes directly into your digestive track. Be aware that this is the most important meal of the day. If you want your body to be healthy and your mind active, please, forget heavy suppers and quick breakfasts of coffee, rolls, and a cigarette. This kind of breakfast indicates a lack of self-regard and self-love.

Also include exercise and daily vitamins: coenzyme Q10 (especially for those older than 40–45), ginkgo biloba, multi-vitamins, proteins, amino acids, anti-oxidants, and oil of evening primrose. You can find all of these in any good health foods store.

1. Preparation: quick and easy!

Red Cream

3 ounces (75 g) of strawberries
1 cup of yogurt
3 tablespoons of milk
Honey
Whipped cream

Conquering Illusions
Red Cream

1. Remove the stems from the strawberries and wash them under a lukewarm faucet. Chop up two of them for garnishing. Blend the rest of them. Add the yogurt, milk, honey, and reblend.
2. Put the mixture in serving cups. Refrigerate for at least 2 hours. Before serving, add a bit of whipped cream on top and garnish with the chopped strawberries that you kept aside.

5 ounces (150 g) of blackberries
1 tablespoon of honey
2 large apples
1 tablespoon of butter
½ teaspoon of cinnamon
Juice of ½ lemon
1 tablespoon of brown sugar

Excitement
Apple Elixir of Sweet Desire

1. Wash the blackberries under a lukewarm faucet. Mix them with the honey and let them marinate for 2 hours.
2. Peel and cut the apples into thin slices. Place them in a baking tin that has been greased with butter. Put the blackberries over the apples and pour the juice left over from the marinade.
3. Add the cinnamon, lemon juice, and brown sugar. Bake for 45 minutes at medium temperature.

1 cup of soy milk
1 tablespoon of wheat germ
2 tablespoons of muesli (whole grain cereal)
1 ounce (30 g) of walnuts or almonds

Cosmic Energy
Buddha's Breakfast

1. Mix 1 cup of soy milk and 1 tablespoon of wheat germ, 2 tablespoons of muesli, and 1 ounce (30 g) of chopped walnuts/almonds.

1 demitasse of mint liqueur
1 tablespoon of brown sugar
½ cup of heavy cream
½ cup of whipped cream
4 fresh, ripe figs
1 sprig of fresh mint

The Middle Path
Nirvana-Drunken Figs

1. Mix the mint liqueur with the brown sugar, heavy cream, and whipped cream. Keep this mix in the refrigerator for at least 2 hours. After this, wash the figs and cut them in half. Put the cream mix in serving cups, sprinkle with chopped, fresh mint. Add the figs and serve.

1 pound (500 g) of brown rice
1 tablespoon ghee or melted butter
Black pepper
Soy sauce
2 ounces (50 g) of grated coconut

Buddhist Purity
Brown Rice with Coconut and Soy

This goes well with green tea.
You can complement rice dishes with *gomashio,* a Japanese condiment prepared from sea salt and toasted sesame seeds.

1. Boil the brown rice.
2. Prepare ghee or melted butter. Add the ghee/melted butter to the cooked rice, along with a sprinkling of black pepper and soy sauce. Sprinkle with the grated coconut.

Buddha's Breakfast

Dates Stuffed with Ricotta Cheese and Honey

15 dates
7 ounces (200 g) of ricotta cheese
5 ounces (150 g) of pistachios
Honey
Cinnamon

A Divine Delicacy

Dates Stuffed with Ricotta Cheese and Honey

1. Slice the dates and remove the pits. Put the ricotta and a pistachio nuts inside. Drizzle with honey and a bit of cinnamon.

15 dates
4 ounces (100 g) of orange
    marmalade
Grated, bittersweet chocolate

Meditation

Dates Stuffed with Orange Marmalade

1. Cut open the dates, fill with 1 teaspoon of orange marmalade and sprinkle with the grated bittersweet chocolate.
You can also heat the chocolate in a water-bath and pour over the dates when melted.

2 egg yolks
2 bulbs of fennel with leaves
Lettuce leaves
Juice of half a lemon
2 tablespoons of oil
1 tablespoon of brown sugar
Salt and pepper, to taste

Inner Movement

Fennel Salad for Sexual Vigor

1. Cook the egg yolks. While they are cooking, clean the fennel bulbs and lettuce and cut them up finely.
2. To prepare the dressing, mix the lemon juice, the oil, the brown sugar, salt and pepper. Mix the cooked egg yolks with the dressing. Pour this over the greens, toss, and cover with a plate. Let it sit for 1 ½ hours before serving.

1 large eggplant
3 tablespoons of flour
2 tablespoons of olive oil
1 clove of garlic (chopped finely)
1 onion (chopped finely)
1 cup of tomato sauce
1 cup of water
2 teaspoons paprika
1 teaspoon of oregano
5 ounces (150 g) of Parmesan cheese
6 ounces (175 g) of mozzarella cheese

Meditation of the Heart

Eggplant with Cheese That Awakens Sensuality

1. Peel and cut the eggplant into thick slices. Dredge the eggplant in the flour and fry in olive oil, along with the chopped onion and garlic, on medium heat until golden.
2. In a bowl, mix the tomato sauce, water, paprika, and oregano. Grease a baking tin with butter, then place the eggplant mix on the bottom, a layer of the sauce over that, and finally layer the cheeses on top of everything.
3. Bake at medium temperature for 15 minutes.

Eggplant with Cheese

12 asparagus
2 eggs
2 tablespoons of butter

Shafts of Light

Aphrodisiac Asparagus

1. Start by boiling the asparagus for 15 minutes. Then drain them and remove the tough (bottom) part of the stalks.
2. Soft boil the eggs for 4 minutes; make sure the white is soft and the yolk still liquid.
3. Serve half of the asparagus for each diner with butter in a small tray or side dish. Serve the eggs in an egg cup. The idea is to dip the asparagus in the butter and then in the egg yolk. You can dip your asparagus in your partner's egg and play erotic games, stimulating both your taste and mouth.

1 cucumber
2 cups (½ l) natural yogurt
1 clove of garlic
2 tablespoons of sugar
1 tablespoon of dill
½ tablespoon of chopped mint
1 tablespoon of olive oil
A pinch of salt
A pinch of black pepper

Dance of Passion

Shiva's Soup

1. Peel the cucumber and cut crosswise into rounds. Mix the cucumber with all the ingredients, except the olive oil, and grind in a food processor. When you have a homogenous mix, put it in the refrigerator and let it chill. Before serving, add the olive oil and mix well.

7 ounces (200 g) of fresh spinach
7 ounces (200 g) of carrots
7 ounces (200 g) of celery stalk
2 eggs
1 large cup of heavy cream
1 pearl onion
½ tablespoon of green
   peppercorns
1 tablespoon of lemon juice
Salt and pepper, to taste

Cosmic Union

Vegetable Pie for Lovers

1. Start off by simmering each of the vegetables separately (you will make each vegetable into its own purée). Do not add too much water so that the purées can be rendered nice and thick. Next, beat the eggs with a bit of the heavy cream, salt and pepper to taste, and add the chopped pearl onion.
2. Add one-third part of the mix to each portion of the vegetables. Blend each portion separately.
3. In a baking tin, put a layer of the carrot purée, then a layer of the celery purée, and finally, the spinach purée. Cook in a water bath for 1 ½ hours. It is a good idea to let the pie cool down a while before you remove it from the tin.
4. Lastly, prepare the dressing that covers the pie. Simmer the remaining heavy cream with the peppercorns, lemon juice, and a pinch of salt. Make this just before you serve the pie.

1 ounce (30 g) of alfalfa sprouts
1 tablespoon of sesame seeds
1 tablespoon of sunflower seeds
1 cup (250 ml) of spring water
2 ounces (55 cc) of ginseng wine
2 tablespoons of honey

Better Than a Love Potion

Elixir of Life

1. In a blender, combine the alfalfa sprouts, the sesame seeds, and sunflower seeds. Blend. Then put the mix in a saucepan with the spring water and gently bring it to a boil.
2. Cover, and let it simmer, slowly, for 30 minutes.
3. Add the ginseng wine (it can be an extract) and the honey.

Recipes That Arouse Passion

Inner Power
Energy Potion

1 pound (½ kg) of carrots
1 stalk of celery
1 sprig of parsley, chopped
A pinch of salt
1 lime
1 grapefruit

1. Chop the carrots, celery, and parsley. Add a pinch of salt and blend. Next, squeeze the lime and grapefruit and add their juices to the above mix. Keep in the refrigerator for ½ hour before serving.

Desire, Passion, and Lust
Hunk o' Burning Artichokes

4 artichokes
Salt and pepper, to taste
A pinch of powdered mustard
2 tablespoons of lemon juice
1 clove of garlic, finely chopped
2 tablespoons of wine vinegar
4 tablespoons of olive oil
2 egg yolks

Artichokes are potently aphrodisiac. This recipe will awaken your sexual desire almost instantly.

1. Remove the toughest petals from the artichokes. Spread the remaining petals and place the artichokes face down, covered with salted water. Cover the pot and let them simmer for 25 minutes. Then drain them and set aside.
2. To prepare the dressing, mix the salt, pepper, mustard, lemon juice, chopped garlic, vinegar, olive oil, and egg yolks. Blend well. Serve the dressing in separate bowls so you can dip the artichoke petals at your leisure.

2 ripe tomatoes
3 tablespoons of chopped parsley
3 tablespoons of Parmesan cheese
2 cloves of garlic, chopped
1 tablespoon of red wine
Salt and pepper, to taste
12 ounces (350 g) of large
    mushrooms
Butter
3 tablespoons of olive oil

Freedom of Mind

Stuffed Mushrooms for the Inhibited

To enjoy good sex we must rid ourselves of preconceived notions that confuse us and alienate us from our desires.

1. Wash and cut up the tomatoes. Mix them with the parsley, Parmesan cheese, chopped garlic, red wine, and salt and pepper to taste.
2. Cut out the stems from the mushroom caps. Fill the caps with the above mix and grease a baking pan with butter.
3. Pour the water and olive oil over the stuffed mushrooms and bake at a medium temperature for 15 minutes.

1 pound (500 g) zucchini
Salt and pepper, to taste
Oregano and marjoram, to taste
¼ cup of pancake batter

Planets, Asteroids, and Meteors in Your Mind

Exquisite Zucchini Fritters

1. Wash and cut the zucchini crosswise into rounds. Season.
2. Dredge the rounds in the pancake batter and fry until golden. Let the fritters sit on paper toweling to absorb any excess oil.

½ tablespoon of saffron
2 cups of chicken broth
6 ounces (175 g) of brown rice
2 ounces (50 g) of chopped green peppers

Tantric Orgasm
Saffron Rice

1. Start by simmering the saffron in the chicken broth. Saffron gives the dish its characteristic taste and delivers the necessary *oomph* for enjoyment. Next, add the brown rice and let it cook on a medium flame. After some 20 minutes the rice will have absorbed all the liquid.
2. Add the chopped green peppers and bake at a medium temperature for 10 minutes.

2 pomegranates
1 tablespoon of rose water
2 cups (½ l) of cold water
Juice of ½ a lemon
3 tablespoons of honey

Kali's Dessert
Red Pomegranates

Even the ancient Egyptians used this delightful concoction to awaken sexual desire (*kundalini*).

1. Peel the pomegranates and remove the seeds. Put them and the rest of the ingredients in a blender and blend. Keep in the refrigerator for 2 hours before serving

Saffron Rice

Stuffed Tomatoes

6 large tomatoes
Salt and pepper
2 cloves of garlic
1 chopped onion
Olive oil
1 pound (½ kg) of ground veal
    or tofu
Cinnamon, saffron, and marjoram
2 ounces (50 g) of pine nuts
2 ounces (50 g) of currants
5 ounces (150 g) of boiled rice
1 sprig of parsley

Making Circles
Stuffed Tomatoes

1. Wash and de-cap the tomatoes; remove the pulp from them. Season and let them sit on a rack for 1 hour. Turn them from time to time. Sauté the garlic and onion in olive oil.
2. Add the ground veal (or tofu) to the garlic and onion with the cinnamon, saffron, marjoram, pine nuts, and currants. Let it cook for 15 minutes.
3. Add the rice, mix, then stuff the tomatoes. Bake at 350° F (180° C) without the caps for a few minutes, and before they are done, put the caps back on. Garnish with parsley and serve.

2 cups of white rice
¼ cup of lukewarm water
½ coconut
1 teaspoon of yeast
Sugar
Salt
2 tablespoons of pre-soaked rice

Peace of Mind
Rice with Grated Coconut

1. Soak the 2 cups of rice for 4 hours. Wash and drain it. Keep 2 tablespoons of the rice aside. Grind the rest of the rice and add a bit of water to form a mash.
2. Let the rice ferment in a bowl with ¼ cup of lukewarm water, a tablespoon of sugar, and teaspoon of yeast.
3. Grind the coconut until it is of liquid consistency. Mix it with the 2 tablespoons of pre-soaked rice and add to the fermenting mix and let it continue to ferment for 6 hours. Add sugar and salt to taste (you can add some coconut milk to adjust the consistency).
4. Bake at 350 ° F (180° C) for 2 hours. Serve it cold.

Cod Croquets

1 pound (½ kg) salted cod fillets
1 pound (500 g) of potatoes
2 ounces (50 g) of butter
1 cup milk
Pepper, to taste
Nutmeg, to taste
4 eggs
1 tablespoon of chopped parsley
5 ounces (150 g) of grated cheese
3 tablespoons of flour
Olive oil
9 ounces (250 g) of bread crumbs
A handful of parsley

Body/Mind Fusion

Cod Croquets

1. De-salt and crumble the cod. Put it in a saucepan with the potatoes (chopped in quarters), the butter, milk, pepper, and nutmeg.
2. Cook covered over a slow fire, then remove and add a whole egg, the yolk of the other egg, parsley, and the grated cheese.
3. Mix well. Refrigerate for 3 hours. Form the croquets and dredge them first in flour, then in 2 beaten eggs with olive oil, and then, finally, in bread crumbs. Fry until golden and put on paper towels to absorb the oil. Garnish with parsley. Serve.

1 pound of garbanzo beans
1 clove
1½ quarts of stock
Olive oil
1 lemon
Salt and pepper
1 cup of cream
5 ounces (150 g) of tahini

The Wheel of Life

Garbanzo Soup

1. Soak the garbanzo beans for a day before you start. Drain the garbanzos and put them in a pot with cold water. Add the clove and simmer on a slow burner for 2 hours.
2. Drain the garbanzos and add 1½ quarts stock. Add the olive oil and lemon. Season to taste.
3. Finally, add the cream and tahini. Serve.

1½ pounds (750 g) of potatoes

2 teaspoons of brown mustard seeds

2 tablespoons of ghee or olive oil

2 cloves of crushed garlic

2 medium onions, sliced

2 tablespoons of fresh, grated ginger

1 teaspoon of ground tumeric

1 teaspoon of ground cumin

½ teaspoon of powdered red chilies

1 teaspoon of garam masala

1 cup of water

5 ounces (150 g) of peas

2 tablespoons of chopped mint

A World Full of Love

Peas and Potato Curry

1. Peel the potatoes and cube them. Toast the mustard seeds in a pan over a medium flame; add the ghee, garlic, onion, and ginger. Remove when the onion is clarified.

2. Add the tumeric, cumin, powdered red chilies, garam masala, and potatoes. Pour in the water and cover, letting it cook until the potatoes start to soften.

3. Mix in the peas, season to taste, and keep covered until the potatoes are done and the liquid is evaporated. Garnish with mint and serve with rice.

1 pound (500 g) of chicken fillets

2 tablespoons of olive oil

2 cloves of garlic, chopped finely

1 piece of grated ginger

2 teaspoons of chopped red chilies

1 pound of cooked jasmine rice, cooled

1 tablespoon of fish sauce

2 teaspoons of golden mountain sauce, or soy sauce

2 ounces (50 g) of chopped basil

2 pearl onions, chopped

½ ounce (15 g) of cilantro leaves

Spiritual Awakening

Chicken and Rice with Cilantro and Ginger

1. Cut up the chicken. Put oil in a frying pan and when hot, sauté the garlic, ginger, and the chopped chilies for 2 minutes. Add the chicken and sauté 3 minutes until it starts to change color.

2. Loosen the rice, add it to the frying pan and mix. When this is good and hot, mix in the fish sauce and golden mountain sauce (or soy sauce) with the basil, pearl onion, and most of the cilantro.

3. Garnish with the remainder of the cilantro and serve.

Peas and Potato Curry

Eden Salad

2 ripe bananas
Juice of 1 lemon
3 ounces (75 g) of chopped celery
2 ounces (50 g) of shelled,
    chopped nuts
A pinch of paprika
Salt, to taste
2 tablespoons of olive oil
2 tablespoons of honey
2 tablespoons of cream cheese
½ teaspoon of powdered ginger

Lovers' Concerto
Banana, Nut, Ginger, and Cheese Salad

1. Peel the bananas and cut them in slices. Sprinkle them with half of the lemon juice so that they don't oxidize and mix them with the chopped celery, nuts, paprika, and salt to taste.
2. Prepare the cheese and ginger dressing that will give the salad an aphrodisiac, finishing touch: mix the oil, honey, cheese, and ginger. Blend together well and pour over the bananas and nuts.

1 lettuce
2 pomegranates (or 10 cherry
    tomatoes)
3 tablespoons of olive oil
Nori or hiziki seaweed, to taste
A pinch each of: black pepper, dill,
    garlic salt, thyme, basil, mint,
    saffron, and paprika
2 tablespoons of vinegar

It's All in the Touch
Eden Salad

1. Mix all the ingredients, except the lettuce and pomegranates (or tomatoes), with 2 tablespoons of water. Stir until you obtain a well-mixed dressing.
2. Chop the lettuce, rinse it, and drain. Put the lettuce in a bowl with the pomegranates or tomatoes (cut in half) and bathe with the dressing.

Sly Celery Salad

2 endives
16 walnuts
1 hard-boiled egg
3 tablespoons of olive oil
½ tablespoon of vinegar
½ teaspoon of tarragon
Salt and pepper, to taste

Staying Alive
Endive of Passion

1. Wash the endive under lukewarm water. Take care to remove any leaves that may be wilted.
2. Chop the walnuts and mix with the endive. Cut up the hard-boiled egg and mix with the rest of the ingredients. Put it all together and mix well.

A stalk of celery
2 pippin apples
1 egg yolk
Salt and pepper, to taste
2 tablespoons of olive oil
½ tablespoon of white rum

Winds of Desire
Sly Celery Salad

1. Wash the celery and cut it into 1 ½ to 2-inch (3-5 cm) pieces. Peel the pippins and cut them into thin slices. Place the apple slices in the middle of a bowl and surround them with the celery. Dress the apple slices with lemon juice so they don't oxidize.
2. Prepare a mayonnaise by first beating the egg yolk with salt and pepper to taste, and then drizzling the olive oil into the beaten egg yolk as you keep stirring. Add the rum to give it a special touch and keep beating until you obtain the desired consistency.

Lettuce leaves
5 ounces (150 g) of Gruyere
    cheese
3 tablespoons of olive oil
1 tablespoon of soy sauce
½ teaspoon of thyme
Salt and pepper, to taste

Naked Bodies

Love Salad

Some cheeses are considered to be aphrodisiac beyond a doubt. This salad is easy and quick to prepare, so much so that you can whip it together in an instant if you have an unexpected guest.

1. Wash the lettuce and chop it. Place it in a bowl and add the Gruyere cheese cut in cubes. Prepare the dressing by adding the soy sauce to the rest of the ingredients and pour over the salad.

½ breast of chicken, cut up
2 ½ cups of water
1 lemon
Salt, to taste
1 onion
Olive oil
1 apple
1 cup of Japanese (round) rice
2 tablespoons of raisins
2 tablespoons of slivered almonds
    or pine nuts
Curry
Salt, to tate

Mix of Flavors

Curried Chicken and Rice

1. Put the cut up chicken breast in the water to cook with a squirt of lemon and salt. Cook until the chicken is tender.
2. Chop the onion finely and sauté in olive oil in a sauce pan until golden in color. When the onions are transparent, add the apple, peeled and cut into cubes, then stir.
3. After a couple of minutes, add the rice, the raisins, and the slivered almonds. Next, add the curry (The quantity will depend on the kind of curry. If it is one of the more classic types, add 1 tablespoon.) Sauté for a few minutes.
4. Add the chicken and its broth and turn up the flame, stirring for a few seconds. Adjust the salt to taste.
   When the broth comes to a boil, lower the flame and let it continue to simmer slowly until the rice is done (about 20 minutes). If the rice on top is still a little hard, cover the sauce pan and let it go a few minutes more.

2 large potatoes, peeled and cubed

1 clove of garlic

2 tablespoons of chopped pearl onions

1 green chili, chopped without seeds

2 tablespoons of ghee or butter

2 pounds (1 kg) of basmati rice

1 teaspoon of sugar

2 teaspoons of garam masala

1 tablespoon of lemon juice

2 tablespoons of chopped cilantro

Black pepper, to season

2 tablespoons of garbanzo flour

1 package of papads (Indian cracker/flatbread), unseasoned*

Olive oil

Mango chutney, to taste

Walking Through the Doors of Life

Potato and Rice Patties

1. Boil the potatoes in salted water until tender. Drain them and purée. Crush the garlic, pearl onion, and the chili together until they form a mash and then fry in ghee, together with the rice that has been previously cooked.

2. Add the sugar, garam masala, potato purée, lemon juice, cilantro, and sprinkle on some pepper. Work this mix until it is homogeneous in texture and form it into patties of a smaller diameter than the *papads*.

3. Make a dough composed of the garbanzo flour and cold water. Let it set up so that it is workable. Take the *papads* and spread the patties of the potato/rice mix over each one. Then take the garbanzo dough, covering over the mix, and press down around the edges with the tines of a fork so as to secure the cover.

4. Heat a bit of olive oil in a pan and fry the patties in batches until they are crisp and golden. Remove them and set on paper towels to absorb any excess oil. Serve them hot and accompany with spicy mango chutney, and garnish with chopped pearl onions or cilantro.

   *The *papads,* and any other ingredients for the recipes of the Hindu gods, are available in stores that sell Oriental products.

1 onion

Olive oil

½ teaspoon of mustard seed

1 teaspoon of *urad dal*

Handful of curry leaves

3 cups of chopped cabbage or collards

½ teaspoon of powdered tumeric

3 cloves of garlic

½ teaspoon of cumin seeds

3 hot green chilies or cayenne peppers

½ cup of coconut

Cosmic Oneness

Spicy Cabbage and Chilies

1. Cut up the onion. Heat a few drops of olive oil in a pan with some mustard seeds; when they pop add the *urad dal* and curry leaves. Then add the onions and sauté until golden.

2. Incorporate the cabbage or collards, tumeric powder, and salt. Stir, lower the heat, cover, and let cook for 5 minutes.

3. Crush the garlic and cumin seeds and add to the pan along with the cayenne pepper and coconut. Stir a few minutes more and remove from the flame.

1 pound (500 g) of green lentils
1 large onion
1 large potato
1 teaspoon of ground cumin
1 teaspoon of ground tumeric
1 teaspoon of ground cilantro
4 ounces (100 g) of flour
Oil for frying
1 tablespoon of grated ginger
2 cloves of chopped garlic
8 ounces (250 g) of tomato purée
1 cup (250 ml) of heavy cream
2 cups of vegetable broth
2 carrots, sliced finely
9 ounces (250 g) of green beans

For the sauce:
1 tablespoon of ghee or oil
1 onion, julienned
1 green chili, chopped
3 teaspoons of fresh ginger, grated
2 cloves of garlic, crushed
1 teaspoon of ground tumeric
3 teaspoons of ground cilantro
1 teaspoon of powdered chili
2 teaspoons of ground cumin
2 tablespoons of white vinegar
1½ cups of coconut milk
2 cups of water
7 ounces (200 g) of yogurt

Inevitable Enlightenment
Lentil Casserole

1. Soak the lentils for 6 hours.
2. Cut the onion and potato in thin slices.
3. Combine and mix well the lentils, potato, cumin, onion, tumeric, cilantro, and flour. Take the mix and form it into small balls the size of a plum and place them in a tray. Cover with aluminum foil. Refrigerate them for 1 hour.
4. In a frying pan, fry the balls in hot oil and after they are golden brown, remove them and place them on absorbent paper toweling to remove all the oil.
5. Heat some oil in a saucepan and sauté the ginger and garlic together for a couple of minutes.
6. Pour in the tomato purée, the heavy cream, and the vegetable broth and mix well. Allow it to simmer uncovered for 10 minutes on a low flame.
7. Add the carrots, lentil balls, and the green beans. Cover and cook on a slow flame for 30 minutes, stirring from time to time.

Lentil Casserole

Belly to Belly

Desserts and Sweets

Beyond Your Wildest Dreams

Magical Plantain Elixir

3 ripe plantains
A pinch of allspice
1 tablespoon of brown sugar
1 cup of water

1. Wash the plantains, but don't peel them. Bake them at low temperature for 25 minutes. Remove the peel and set aside the pulp.
2. Grate the inside of the peels and mix with the allspice and brown sugar. Boil the water and add this mix to it. Stir until it caramelizes.
   This plantain elixir (a powerful aphrodisiac) is wonderful to pour over a fruit salad!

The Heat of Desire

Belly to Belly

2 ounces (50 g) of crushed, dried rose petals
2 cups of almond milk
½ tablespoon of cinnamon
½ tablespoon of ginger
2 tablespoons of rice flour
2 tablespoons of cold water
4 ounces (100 g) of pitted, chopped dates
3 tablespoons of pine nuts
Handful of fresh rose petals

1. This powerful aphrodisiac will ignite your passion. Soak the dried, crushed rose petals in the almond milk. After 10 minutes, add the cinnamon and ginger and stir well.
2. Cook on a low flame for 5 minutes and incorporate the rice flour and 2 tablespoons of cold water. Add the dates and pine nuts and stir.
   Serve this dish lukewarm and garnished with the fresh rose petals.

4 ripe mangos
½ tablespoon of sugar
1 cup of milk
A pinch of black pepper

Hands on Hips
Sensual Dessert

1. Peel the mangoes and remove the pits. Blend the fruit with the sugar and milk in a blender.
2. All you need to do is add the black pepper and you are ready to enjoy this recipe that is one of the aphrodisiacs of the East.

8 ounces of shelled walnuts
1 cup of goat's milk
2 tablespoons of honey
4 egg yolks

Sweet Encounter
Walnut Cream

1. Crush the walnuts and heat them in the goat's milk on a slow flame so as to blanch them. Next, beat this with the honey and egg yolks. This dessert will stimulate ardent passion if you serve it well-chilled, accompanied with a sweet liqueur.

6 dates
6 dried figs
1 tablespoon of licorice root
2 tablespoons of honey
½ tablespoon of cinnamon
½ melon

An Artist's Heart
Fruit Smoothie

1. Chop the dates, dried figs, and licorice root.
2. Simmer the above for 15 minutes over a low flame. Remove from the fire and add the honey, cinnamon, and melon (chopped).
3. Put in a blender and blend. Serve immediately.

2 pomegranates
2 tablespoons of chopped almonds
1 tablespoon of sesame seeds
1 tablespoon of pine nuts
1 tablespoon of sake (rice wine)

Literary Fame
Pomegranate and Nuts Delight

1. Peel the pomegranates and put aside. Chop the almonds, pine nuts, and sesame, then mix in a bowl. Crush the pomegranate and add to the nuts.
2. Pour the sake into the mix and blend it. Serve this wonderful elixir well-chilled.

½ fresh papaya
1 tablespoon of lemon juice
2 tablespoons of white rum
2 tablespoons of brown sugar
1 cup of crushed ice

Cult of the Goddess
Divine Nectar of Papaya

1. Peel the papaya and remove the seeds. Cut it in small pieces and mix with the rest of the ingredients. Serve in cocktail glasses. (See photo on page 2.)

4 egg yolks
3 tablespoons of brown sugar
2 ounces (50 g) of fresh ginger
8 ounces (225 g) of chestnut purée
4 tablespoons of orange liquor
1 tablespoon of lemon juice
2 cups (½ l) heavy cream

Carving Your Statue
Chestnut and Ginger Delights

1. Beat the egg yolks with the brown sugar. Chop the ginger finely and add it to the yolks along with the chestnut purée, the orange liquor, and the lemon juice.
2. Add the heavy cream and mix well. Put in the refrigerator. Serve this dessert well-chilled.

1 small pineapple
1 kiwi
1 mango
1 passion fruit
1 banana
2 tablespoons of cane sugar
1 tablespoon of white rum

Goose Bumps/Mystical Heart
Cup of Paradise

1. Remove the pulp from the pineapple, making sure not to break the rind. Peel all the fruits, except the passion fruit, and cut them in cubes of more-or-less equal size.
2. Put the cubed fruit back in the pineapple shell. Next, simmer the mango pit with the sugar, rum, and the crushed pulp of the passion fruit. Remove the pit from the syrup and pour the syrup over the fruit in the pineapple shell.

4 apples
2 cups (500 ml) of red wine
1 ounce (30 g) of sugar
1 demitasse of rose liqueur
1 clove

Forever Embrace
Apples in Rose Liqueur

1. Peel and core the apples. Simmer the red wine with the sugar, the rose liqueur, and the cloves. Add the apples and let cook for 10 minutes on a slow flame. Check the apples with a fork to see if they are tender.
2. Put in a salad bowl, add more wine, and chill for 2 hours.

2 ounces (55 g) of yellow ginseng root
1 ounce (25 g) of ginger root, sliced
honey, to taste

Explosion of Passion
Ginseng, Ginger, and Honey

1. Cook the ginger and ginseng for 45 minutes on a low flame. Sweeten with honey: the best would be from orange blossoms, rosemary blossoms, or eucalyptus blossoms.

1 pound of chopped Pine
   mushrooms *(Lactarius deliciosus)*
1 clove of garlic
Parsley and sage
1 quart water
Sea salt, to taste
11 ounces (300 g) of cornmeal
1 ounce (30 g) of butter
7 ounces of Emmentaler cheese,
   grated

Dazzling Heights of Love
Mushroom and Polenta Pie

1. Lightly season the Pine mushrooms with garlic, parsley, and sage, and put them to boil in a quart (1 liter) of water salted with sea salt. Next, cook cornmeal separately for 5 minutes over a low flame, stirring continually.
2. Grease a baking tin with a bit of butter. Put half the polenta in the bottom, then pour in the mushroom mixture, add part of the grated Emmentaler cheese, and cover with the rest of the cornmeal. Next, put the remainder of the cheese on top and some of the sage leaves.
3. Bake for 25 minutes, and let it sit for 5 minutes before serving. Accompany with escarole or lettuce and pomegranate.

5 level tablespoons of cornstarch
1 cup water
12 ounces (350 g) sugar
2 cups (500 ml) of milk
2 tablespoons of butter
3 eggs
1 teaspoon of powdered vanilla
12 ounces (350 g) frozen fillo
   dough

For the syrup:
5 ounces (125 g) of sugar
3 tablespoons of water
1 lemon

Bound by Desire
Fillo Pastry (*Galatuboureki*)

1. Defrost the fillo dough and separate the leaves. Mix the cornstarch in a cup of water and add half of the sugar with a pinch of salt. Heat up the milk and add the cornstarch/sugar mix gradually, constantly stirring with a wooden spoon as you go. When the milk thickens sufficiently, remove from the flame and add the butter. Beat the eggs with the other half of the sugar. Add the vanilla to the eggs and sugar. Gradually stir in the liquid mixture, stirring continually. Cover and chill.
2. Grease a rectangular baking tray with butter. Use a rolling pin to spread the fillo leaves on a flat surface. Make two layers of fillo leaves (one for the top and one for the bottom) and grease them with melted butter on both sides. Set the oven to 350° F (180° C).
3. Form one of the fillo layers on the bottom of the baking tray and pour the cream filling on it. Cover with the second layer of leaves. Cut the pie with a knife, making diamond-shaped pieces. Make sure to cut through to the bottom of the pan. Brush melted butter onto the top of the pie and moisten with a bit of cold water. Put in the oven for about 45 minutes (until the top is golden brown).
4. Grate the lemon skin and squeeze out the juice. Heat the water and add the sugar and lemon peel. Keep on a low flame. Let it simmer for 5 minutes until it turns into a syrup, then remove from the heat and add the lemon juice.
   When the pie is done, carefully pour the hot syrup over it.

Chocolate and Dried Fruit Truffles

Mayan and Aztec Recipes

Chocolate Temptations

Dance of the Snake
Chocolate Meringue

2 scoops of vanilla ice cream
½ ounce (15 g) of chopped dark chocolate
4 meringue nests
2 tablespoons of cream of mint
2 tablespoons of grated milk chocolate

1. Take the vanilla ice cream out of the freezer a half hour before starting the recipe. Mix the ice cream with the chopped dark chocolate and place it in the meringue nests.
2. Pour the cream of mint on top and garnish with the grated milk chocolate.

Sacred Memory
Chocolate and Nut Truffles

4 ounces (125 g) of bittersweet chocolate
2 ounces (50 g) of walnuts
1 ounce (25 g) of pistachios
1 ounce (25 g) of almonds
1 tablespoon of butter
2 tablespoons of powdered sugar
2 tablespoons of powdered cocoa

1. Crush the nuts into small bits, without making them into powder. Melt the bittersweet chocolate and butter into a saucepan, and add the nuts and sugar. Mix well and remove from the flame. When it cools, form it into little balls and roll them in the powdered cocoa.

Spiritual Liberation
Chocolate Pears in Ginger

4 pears
6 tablespoons of brown sugar
1 piece of ginger root
7 ounces (200 g) of chocolate fondant

1. Peel the pears, but do not remove the stem. Boil them with the sugar and ginger root. Stir from time to time.
2. After 15 minutes, strain the pears and let them cool. Just before you put them on a plate, melt the chocolate fondant and pour it over the pears.

2 cups of water
Several sprigs of fresh mint
4 tablespoons of sugar
4 ounces (100 g) of bittersweet chocolate
1 demitasse of apple liqueur

Return of the Master
Chocolate Nest

1. Make a mint infusion first. Bring water to a boil, then turn down the heat. Add the mint and let it steep for 5 minutes, without boiling it, since the mint will lose its properties if it does. Strain.
2. Add the sugar and chocolate and stir until they dissolve. Add the apple liqueur. Remove the mixture from the heat and let it cool. Put it in the freezer for 3 hours. Stir it from time to time.
Serve the sorbet in cocktail cups and garnish with mint leaves.

5 ounces (150 g) of dried figs
4 ounces (125 g) of walnuts
4 ounces (125 g) of almonds
3 ounces (100 g) of pistachios
5 ounces (150 g) of sugar
3 tablespoons of powdered cocoa

Mystic Call
Dried Fruit Bonbons

1. Crush all the ingredients, minus the cocoa, until you obtain a homogeneous paste. Form the paste into balls and roll them in the powdered cocoa.
These bonbons are an aphrodisiac delight of dried fruit and chocolate.

1 cup of water
3 ounces (100 g) of sugar
3 ounces (100 g) of bittersweet chocolate
4 egg yolks
½ tablespoon of allspice
1 tablespoon of coffee
2 tablespoons of Benedictine liqueur
3 cups of heavy cream

The Impulse of Life
Chocolate Benedictine

Chocolate and Benedictine liqueur (a delicious, aromatic secret formulation made by the monks of the Abby of Fécamp, France) are a powerful mix for waking up sexual desire.

1. Boil the water and add the sugar. Lower the heat and stir until the sugar dissolves. Meanwhile, melt the chocolate in a water bath and beat it together with the egg yolks, allspice, and then the sugar syrup.
2. When it cools down, add the coffee, the Benedictine, and the heavy cream. Mix, and let it chill in the refrigerator before serving.

Chocolate Nest

For the soufflés (makes 10):

1 pod of vanilla
1 cup (250 ml) of milk
5 ounces (150 g) baking chocolate
4 ounces (125 g) of butter
4 ounces (125 g) of flour
Whites of 8 eggs
8 egg yolks
3 ounces (70 g) of toasted, ground
    walnuts
4 ounces (100 g) of sugar
Butter and sugar for the baking
    molds
10 molds, 1 cup (200 ml) capacity

For topping:

Powdered sugar

Chocolate on Chocolate

Mini Chocolate Soufflés

1. Slit the vanilla pod lengthwise and take out the inside. Put the pod and the seeds in milk and heat. Melt the baker's chocolate in a water bath.
2. Melt the butter in a saucepan, add the flour and let it brown a bit. Remove the vanilla pod from the milk and pour it into the flour and butter in the saucepan. Keep it on a low flame for 10 minutes and stir constantly.
3. Strain the mixture. Let it cool briefly, then add two egg whites without beating. Next, add the egg yolks, one by one, stirring until you obtain a perfectly even consistency. Now add the melted chocolate and nuts.
4. Whisk the remaining egg whites with the sugar until stiff. Incorporate ¼ of this meringue into the batter, mixing it with a hand beater. Carefully add the remainder with a spatula.
5. Grease the molds and dust with sugar. Using a pastry bag with a wide nozzle, fill the molds to ¾ full (the batter will rise in the oven).
6. Place the molds in a water bath and bake for 20 minutes in an oven pre-heated to 350° F (180° C). The center of the soufflés should remain somewhat liquid (check them with a toothpick).

Before serving, remove the soufflés from the molds and dust with powdered sugar.

Mini Chocolate Soufflés

This recipe will make approximately 12 tortillas:

2 cups of wheat flour
½ cup of water

Circular Universe
Mexican Tortillas

1. Put the flour in a bowl and slowly add the water to form a pliant dough that can be rolled into a ball.
It is very important that you knead the dough well, since this will allow the tortillas to rise and cook evenly.
Let the dough sit for 10 minutes.

2. Roll the dough into 12 even-sized balls. Let them sit covered with a cloth for 5 minutes.
Dust your working table with flour and flatten each ball until it is quite thin, about 1/8 of an inch thick (3 mm).
Add more flour if needed. It will be a lot easier if you use plastic wrap to make the tortillas. Dust the wrap, place the balls on it, then cover the balls with another sheet of plastic and flatten them. This will help to prevent the tortillas from breaking when you handle them.

3. Heat a frying pan; do not use any butter or oil. Cook the tortillas for 1 minute on one side, then 1 minute on the other side. You can flip the tortilla when it starts to inflate. Continue cooking it a couple of minutes more. The tortilla should be flexible in consistency, without browning or toasting it. When done, put the tortilla on a towel so that it keeps warm. Try to serve them hot, or at least warm.

Important: Don't put salt in the dough, since the complements of the tortillas are already quite spicy!

2 pounds (1 kg) of guava fruit
1 ½ pounds (750 g) of sugar
5 tablespoons of water

Inner Riches
Guava Pearls

1. Wash the guavas and remove the black bud. Cut the guavas in half. Take out the cores (with the seeds) and save them.
2. Cut the flesh of each guava into 4 pieces and put them in a pot or saucepan with the sugar on a medium flame. Stir constantly. Put the cores in a juicer with the water, so as to remove the seeds. Strain the remaining pulp and add to the pot. Let the mix thicken into a paste, allowing the liquid to evaporate.
3. Next day, form the paste into small balls and, if you would like to increase the sweetness, coat them with sugar or honey.

1 cup of cooked kidney beans
⅓ cup of water, or the broth left over from cooking the beans
¼ cup of olive oil
4 corn tortillas
2 cups of queso fresco or queso manchego (La Mancha Cheese)
3 tablespoons of chopped onion
1 chili pepper
½ cup of cream for dressing

Cause and Effect
Frijoles (Beans)

1. Heat the oil, add the beans and mash them. Add the broth (or water) and cook. Put a corn tortilla in the beans and leave it for 10 seconds, then flip it and let it sit another 10 seconds.
2. Remove the tortilla and stuff it with cheese, onion, and (if you like) chili pepper, and roll it up.
   Do the same with all the tortillas.
   Serve them hot, and add more cheese on top and a bit of cream.

1 small onion, finely chopped

1 tablespoon of olive oil

2 finely chopped tomatoes

A big bunch of spinach, chopped finely

Salt and pepper, to taste

1 pound (500 g) of cornmeal dough (masa)

4 ounces (100 g) of margarine

5 ounces of yeast

7 ounces (200 g) of queso fresco (adobera)

10 tamale leaves (soaked and drained), or aluminum foil to wrap the tamales

5 ounces (150 g) of cream, for dressing the tamales

Spinach and Cheese Tamales

1. Sauté the onion in oil, add the tomatoes and spinach. Season with salt and pepper. Let it cool down.
2. Knead the cornmeal by hand, or use a mixer. Add the margarine and salt and mix well. Add the yeast and cheese, keep beating and add the cooked spinach and adjust the salt.
3. Into the sheets of aluminum foil (or tamale leaves), put 3 tablespoons of cornmeal dough (masa) and fold the sides of the sheets/leaves toward the center, and the lower flap upward.

   Steam for approximately 1 ½ hours.

   Serve hot, covered with tomato sauce and cream. Accompany with cooked beans.

10 ounces (300 g) of mushrooms

1 teaspoon of chicken consommé

1 large tomato, cubed

½ onion, finely chopped

½ cup of tomato puree

Juice of 2 lemons

1 tablespoon of soy sauce

1 hot chili pepper, fresh and diced

2 sprigs of cilantro, washed and chopped

Salt, to taste

Heaven and Earth

Mushroom Cocktail

1. Wash the mushrooms and cut in slices. Simmer them in a cup of boiling water.
2. Add the chicken consommé and let cool. Mix all the ingredients in a large bowl.

   Serve this as an entrée in cups or dessert dishes. You can accompany it with crackers: it is delicious!

3 hot chilies without seeds or tops,
  cooked
Salt, to taste
1 clove of garlic
½ cup of vinegar
4 small tomatoes, cooked
1 tablespoon of oregano
1 cup of olive oil
1 pound (500 g) of thin corn
  tortillas
1 cup of *queso fresco*
Onion slices, to taste
½ head of lettuce, finely chopped
4 radishes
Salsa, for garnish

2 large zucchini
1 chive
2 carrots
1 red pepper
Olive oil
Black pepper

For the béchamel sauce:
1 tablespoon of olive oil
1 tablespoon of flour
Vegetable broth
Salt

The Flavor of Life
Spicy Enchiladas

1. Mash the cooked chilies with a bit of salt, the garlic, and vinegar. Run them through a strainer and place in a deep dish. Mash the tomatoes with the oregano and salt to taste. Heat oil in a large saucepan.
2. Rub the tortillas in the chili mix, then fry them, one by one.
3. Fill the tortillas with cheese and a touch of onion, roll up to serve. Serve them hot, with lettuce and radishes, and pour the salsa on top.

"In Lakesh": I Am Another You
Vegetable Lasagna

1. Cut the zucchini in crosswise slices (rounds), as thin as possible. Cut the rest of the vegetables as you prefer; it's interesting to note how each has its own form and density.
2. In a baking tray, greased with olive oil, alternate a layer of zucchinis with a layer of the other vegetables. It works best if you layer the different vegetables separately: onion in one layer, red peppers in another, carrots in another.
3. Lightly season each layer as it is put down. It is a good idea to drizzle a bit of olive oil every other layer to give added taste.
   Put in the oven at medium temperature. Baking time depends on the thickness of the lasagna and its layers. It works best if the individual layers and the lasagna itself are on the thin side. At any rate, cooking time will exceed ½ hour.
4. While the lasagna is baking, prepare a béchamel sauce by putting the olive oil in a saucepan and lightly toasting the flour. Add, bit by bit, the vegetable broth and salt to taste. Keep stirring as you add a small amount of broth at a time. The total amount of broth you add depends on how thick you want the béchamel to be. When the lasagna is done, pour the béchamel sauce on top of it.

Vegetable Lasagna

Challah
Bread

Miscellaneous Recipes

Bread, Fish, and Lamb

½ ounce (15 g) of fresh baker's
  yeast
3 tablespoons of water
1 tablespoon of sugar
14 ounces (400 g) of pastry flour
1 teaspoon of fine salt
2 ounces of whipped butter (not
  liquid)
2 eggs (separate yolks from whites)
2 tablespoons of poppy seeds

Raising of Spirit
Challah Bread

1. In a bowl, mix the yeast, water, and sugar. Cover and let it ferment until bubbles appear on the surface. Sift the flour and salt into a large bowl and make a hollow in the center for the yeast/water/sugar mix. Add the butter and the egg yolks (keep the whites aside). Add 1 demitasse extra of water. Mix uniformly with a spatula until a soft ball is formed. It should not be sticky; if necessary, add flour bit-by-bit to obtain the desired consistency.

2. On a clean surface, dusted with flour, work the dough until it is smooth and spongy. Keep it in a bowl that has been lightly oiled (use sunflower or corn oil) at room temperature until it doubles in volume.

3. When the dough has risen sufficiently, knead it again for about 5 minutes. Cover the dough ball with a clean, moist cloth and let it sit another 5 minutes. Next divide the dough into 3 equal portions and form them into braids about 12 inches (30 cm) long. Twist the three braids together and pinch the ends into a single point, so the bread doesn't unravel when baked. Put the braided dough into a tray greased with butter and cover, again, with a clean, moist cloth and let it double in size.

4. Preheat the oven to 430° F. (220° C.). Mix the egg whites with 1 tablespoon of water and, using a clean brush, paint the whole surface of the bread with this mixture. Put the bread in the oven and bake for 10 minutes. Remove it and recoat with the egg white and water mix, sprinkle with the poppy seeds and return the loaf to the oven, covered with aluminum foil. Bake for another 30 minutes.
The bread is done if it sounds hollow when you tap it on the bottom.

10 ounces (270 g) of flour
6 ounces (180 g) of semolina
1 ½ teaspoons of salt
1 cup of mineral water
Toasted sesame seeds

Spiritual Advancement
Unleavened Bread (Matzo)

1. About 40 minutes before baking, preheat the oven to 270° F. (130° C.). Mix the flour, semolina, and salt in a bowl, add the water bit-by-bit until you form a soft dough. Form the dough into a ball and place on a floured surface. Knead for 1 minute.
2. The dough should be firm, elastic, but not sticky. Divide into 12 balls, about 2 ounces (50 g) each and cover them with a clean, moist cloth.
3. Take a ball and flatten it into a disk about 4 inches (10 cm) in diameter, then roll it out to 9 inches (23 cm). Exact measurement is not the point here; what is important is that the disk is very thin, transparent when held in your hand.
4. When the disks are done, sprinkle them with the toasted sesame and fix the seeds by rolling over them.
5. Put in the oven and bake for about 3 minutes, just until they start to turn golden in color. Turn them over using tongs, and let the other side turn golden as well.

According to tradition, when the Israelites fled ancient Egypt, they didn't have time to prepare leavened bread, hence matzo. Unleavened bread is made without yeast. Its dough is prepared with flour and water, to which salt can be added. One can form it into whatever shape one wishes, before putting it in the oven. Wheat, barley, corn, and other cereals are used to make the flour. For a long time, unleavened bread was the only kind known to humanity.

Matzo is prepared with unrefined flour, that is to say whole wheat, and it is baked over hot bricks or ashes. Most recently, unleavened bread has evolved into myriad varieties of bread that we are familiar with today, such as pita bread or ciabatta. This evolution is due to the development of the oven, the use of leavening, refinement of cereal flours, and adding various ingredients such as olives, butter, spices, etc.

Homemade Bread

To make 2 pounds (1 kg) of bread:

1 ½ pounds (750 g) of flour
1 ounce (30 g) of baker's yeast
½ tablespoon of salt
2 cups of lukewarm water
A pinch of sugar

1. Sift the flour and salt into a big bowl. If you are going to use sugar, first mix it with the yeast and lukewarm water, then incorporate it into the flour. Keep mixing until you achieve a firm, sticky dough. Clean a work area, for example, the countertop, and dust it with flour. Take the dough and knead it until it is elastic and appears glossy. When the dough is ready, form it into a ball and put it back in the bowl.

2. Cover the dough with transparent film wrap and let it sit until it doubles in volume (depending on temperature and humidity, this will take between 1 and 2 hours). To test if the dough is ready: press into it with a finger and if the hollow stays for a few moments, it is done. Next, knead it once more and form it into a ball and cover it with a cloth. Let the dough sit for another 15 minutes. Avoid a drafty, cold work surface.

3. After the 15 minutes, reform the dough into a ball and cover it with the cloth. Let the dough double in volume again; this will take about 1 hour. After this, you are ready to prepare it for baking. Make the dough into the shape you desire for the loaf and make a few cuts on the surface with a knife, to your liking. Preheat the oven to 425° F. (220° C.) and put a small bowl (ovenproof!) with some water to keep the humidity.

4. Put the loaf in the oven. After 20 minutes, remove the bowl of water and let it bake another 15 minutes. Reduce the oven temperature to 375° F. (190 C.) and keep it there until the bread is done. If you want a loaf a bit more "rustic," add some rye, or barley, or whole wheat flour in place of all white flour. If you can bake the loaf in a wood-fired oven, so much the better!

The ingredients for making bread are simple, requiring just flour, yeast, water, and salt. You've probably thought of making bread at one time or another and here you have the simplest recipe to do so. Let the loaf cool on a rack and keep it in an airtight container so it keeps for a few days. You will have a bread with bubbles and air pockets, interesting in texture and very crusty. This dough, spread not too thin, can also be used for making pizza.

9 toasted hazelnuts
1 slice of fried bread
1 onion
2 cloves of garlic
2 cups (½ liter) of white wine
1 pound (500 g) of de-salted cod
  (bacalao), cut up
7 ounces (200 g) of garbanzo
  beans
7 ounces (200 g) of green beans
1 bouillon cube
Oil, saffron, parsley, and salt

We Are All One

Cod with Green Beans and Garbanzos

1. Grind the toasted hazelnuts with the fried bread in a mortar. Finely chop and sauté the onion and garlic together.
2. In an earthenware casserole put oil, the wine, and the pieces of cod and let it cook, covered, until it is tender. Stir it from time to time.
3. Add the garbanzos, the green beans (previously boiled and cut into thin slices), the contents of the mortar, the bouillon cube, chopped parsley, and some saffron petals. Mix all, and sauté for a few minutes.

12 ounces (350 g) of lamb
  shoulder, cubed
2 tablespoons of olive oil
3 cloves of garlic
½ teaspoon of dry rub seasoning
1 cup of water
3 ounces (75 g) of lentils
1 cup of broth
½ teaspoon of thyme
¼ teaspoon of rosemary
1 demitasse of goat yogurt
A pinch of fresh mint

Passionately

Three Spices Lamb

1. Begin by sautéing the lamb in the olive oil. Next add a clove of garlic, finely chopped, and the dry rub seasoning.
2. Add the water and cook until the meat is tender. Separately, cook the lentils in the broth. Add the rest of the garlic (chopped) and the herbs. Incorporate this into the lamb and let cook on a slow flame for 25 minutes.
   Serve hot, mixed with the goat yogurt and garnished with the fresh mint.

Cod with Green Beans and Garbanzos

1 ounce (30 g) of baker's yeast
½ can condensed milk
1 egg
2 ounces (50 g) of melted butter
Grated lemon peel
1 teaspoon of vanilla essence
11 ounces (300 g) of flour

For the custard:

3 egg yolks
½ can condensed milk
2 tablespoons of cornstarch
1 squirt of vanilla essence
Granulated sugar, walnuts, or
  chopped almonds

Circle of Glory

Easter Bread

Making the Dough:

1. Dissolve the yeast in lukewarm water with a pinch of sugar. Add the condensed milk, the egg, the melted butter, the grated lemon peel, and essence of vanilla. Beat for 5 minutes.
2. Add flour to the above and mix until you can form it into a ball. Take the ball and knead it. Put the ball in a bowl, cover it with a cloth, and let it sit in a warm place for an hour.
3. When the hour is up, take the dough and make a hollow in the center of the ball with your hand. Insert a buttered, floured, round cutter in this hollow (cut through and take out the center, leave the cutter in place) and let the dough rise another 2 hours on a buttered, floured tray.

Making the Custard:

1. In a saucepan, mix the egg yolks with the condensed milk, cornstarch, and water. Stir constantly as you heat over a slow flame. When it starts to boil, stir more rapidly and turn off the heat.
2. Keep stirring until the mix cools down and add the vanilla essence. Pour over the dough.
3. Brush the dough and custard with beaten egg. Sprinkle with granulated sugar and the almonds or walnuts and bake at medium temperature for 30 minutes.

3 quarts milk
3 cups sugar
lemon peel
cinnamon stick
1½ rice, cooked

Open Heart

Rice and Milk

1. In a saucepan, combine the milk, sugar, lemon peel, and cinnamon stick. Bring to a boil, stirring constantly.
2. Put cooked rice in separate bowl and pour in milk mixture. Garnish with the lemon strips and sprinkle with cinnamon powder.

Easter Bread

CONVERSION CHARTS
METRIC AND IMPERIAL CONVERSIONS
(These conversions are rounded for convenience)

Ingredient	Cups/Tablespoons/ Teaspoons	Ounces	Grams/Milliliters
Butter	1 cup = 16 tablespoons = 2 sticks	8 ounces	230 grams
Cheese, shredded	1 cup	4 ounces	110 grams
Cream cheese	1 tablespoon	0.5 ounce	14.5 grams
Cornstarch	1 tablespoon	0.3 ounce	8 grams
Flour, all-purpose	1 cup/1 tablespoon	4.5 ounces/0.3 ounce	125 grams/8 grams
Flour, whole wheat	1 cup	4 ounces	120 grams
Fruit, dried	1 cup	4 ounces	120 grams
Fruits or veggies, chopped	1 cup	5 to 7 ounces	145 to 200 grams
Fruits or veggies, puréed	1 cup	8.5 ounces	245 grams
Honey, maple syrup, or corn syrup	1 tablespoon	.75 ounce	20 grams
Liquids: cream, milk, water, or juice	1 cup	8 fluid ounces	240 milliliters
Oats	1 cup	5.5 ounces	150 grams
Salt	1 teaspoon	0.2 ounce	6 grams
Spices: cinnamon, cloves, ginger, or nutmeg (ground)	1 teaspoon	0.2 ounce	5 milliliters
Sugar, brown, firmly packed	1 cup	7 ounces	200 grams
Sugar, white	1 cup/1 tablespoon	7 ounces/0.5 ounce	200 grams/12.5 grams
Vanilla extract	1 teaspoon	0.2 ounce	4 grams

OVEN TEMPERATURES

Fahrenheit	Celsius	Gas Mark
225°	110°	$1/4$
250°	120°	$1/2$
275°	140°	1
300°	150°	2
325°	160°	3
350°	180°	4
375°	190°	5
400°	200°	6
425°	220°	7
450°	230°	8